Paul and His Christian Mission

Includes Study Guide

PAUL
AND HIS CHRISTIAN
MISSION

Michael Azad A.G. Haykin

Includes Study Guide

HERITAGE
SEMINARY
PRESS

Heritage Seminary Press, Cambridge, Ontario
An imprint of H&E Publishing, Peterborough, Ontario, Canada

hesedandemet.com

Cover and book design by Janice Van Eck
Study guide by Janice Van Eck

Front cover: This image of Paul writing comes from an early ninth-century manuscript, written in the Monastery of Saint Gall (St. Gallen), Switzerland, now housed in Württembergische Landesbibliothek, Stuttgart. This is believed to be one of the earliest depictions of the apostle Paul in a European manuscript. It follows an early medieval tradition of depicting the author of a text as seated and writing. The inscription says: *S(AN)C(TU)S PAULUS sedet hic scripsit* ("Saint Paul sits here [and] writes"). *Wikimedia Commons*

Paul and His Christian Mission
Michael Azad A.G. Haykin

ISBN 978-1-77484-106-8   (Paperback)
ISBN 978-1-77484-107-5   (Ebook)

In thankful memory of

Bruce Woods (1931–2022),
a Pauline father in Christ

&

Richard N. Longenecker (1930–2021),
a Pauline scholar *par excellence*

Contents

Preface

This book on the Christian mission of the apostle Paul origi-
nated in a series of talks given in July 2011 at Muskoka Bible
Centre in the Muskokas, Ontario. I am deeply thankful to its
director, John Friesen, for the privilege of speaking on that occasion, and indeed, for a longstanding involvement in the summer
ministry of this remarkable Christian endeavour.

My first time on the grounds of Muskoka Baptist Conference
(what Muskoka Bible Centre was then called) was in the summer
of 1977. My wife Alison and I had been married in November of
the previous year at Stanley Avenue Baptist Church, Hamilton, by
Pastor Bruce Woods. The following summer, Bruce's eldest son,
Mark Woods, and his wife Shelley invited Alison and me, along with
another couple of friends, Peter and Sandy Fodor, to join them on a
canoe trip in Algonquin Park. We were to meet at the Woods' cottage,
which was on the grounds of the Muskoka Baptist Conference. We
stayed just a few hours at the cottage, but it was the beginning of
a long love affair with this part of Ontario.

Given this book's link with Muskoka Bible Centre, it is appropriate that one of those to whom I dedicate this book is Bruce
Woods; I owe him an enormous debt. I came to Christ under his
ministry at Stanley Avenue Baptist Church in 1974. He baptized
me in April of that year and gave me opportunities to teach and
speak publicly at the church. He gave me sage advice on theological matters such as the work of the Holy Spirit and eschatology.
(He had been to Dallas Theological Seminary but was moving

away from classical Dispensationalism.) When I sensed a call to vocational ministry in the church at the time of my conversion, he very wisely encouraged me to go to Wycliffe College, which was such a blessing in so many ways. He officated at my wedding, as noted above, and when I finished seminary, he played a key role in helping me get a teaching position at Central Baptist Seminary in 1982. When I decided to go to Southern Baptist Theological Seminary full-time in 2006, his was one of two voices of counsel I consulted; the other was Bob Holmes. I treasured Bruce's advice, as I knew he approached the matter without bias. In later years, we would meet for tea/coffee at Tim Hortons near his home in Ancaster, Ontario. (Ancaster is right next door to Dundas, where I live.) These meetings were always a joy. I loved his sanguine outlook on and zest for life, his zeal for Christ and winsome boldness in sharing his faith, his creativity and fearlessness and his Pauline passion for the spread of the kingdom of Christ. I shall be forever grateful to God for his deep impact upon my life.

Indeed, it was under Woods' ministry that I first learned about the apostle Paul, who, undoubtedly, is one of the most influential thinkers in Western culture.[1] In what follows, we shall explore six aspects of Paul's missionary passion. The books on this area of the life of the apostle Paul are literally legion. Two have been especially important to me. First, there is Eckhard J. Schnabel's *Paul the Missionary,* which I consider the definitive modern monograph on this subject. Then, there is an older study, which did much to shape my early thinking about Paul's ministry: F.F. Bruce's *Paul: Apostle of the Heart Set Free,* a superb work based on a lifetime of study of the Pauline texts and the Lukan account of Paul's mission in Acts.

One Pauline scholar whose lectures and seminars also profoundly shaped my reading of Paul and his mission was Richard N. Longenecker (1930–1921). When Pastor Woods encouraged me to attend Wycliffe College, little did I know the remarkable scholars under whom I would study. One of them, who taught me

---

1 I am indebted for this thought to the comment by Douglas A. Campbell: "Paul is the most influential political philosopher in the USA today, and arguably in the rest of the world as well, and this surely makes him one of the most important figures in human history" (*Paul: An Apostle's Journey* [Grand Rapids, MI: William B. Eerdmans Publ. Co., 2018], 1).

most of my New Testament courses, was Dr. Longenecker.[2] I was but twenty when I began my studies under him, far too young in many ways to appreciate the remarkable scholar that he was, not only in terms of learning but also in terms of character.[3] The passing years have deepened my appreciation of having been tutored by such a fine Pauline scholar, who not only taught me about Paul's thought but also modeled how to be a Christian scholar.

In this book, I explore six aspects of Paul's mission that were essential to its success. These six aspects of the Pauline mission lie at the very foundation of the church in the Mediterranean basin, a key matrix of Christianity. First, there is his focus on conversion, which, in turn, is grounded in the dominical commissioning of Paul to go to the Gentiles "to open their eyes." Then, there is the way Paul's mission was tied very much to his love for the people of God. Third, Paul was also an activist, who maintained an evangelistic zeal at white-hot flame all his life. Fourth, Paul knew that without prayer his mission would come to nothing. Moreover, at the heart of the Pauline mission was what scholars call the Pauline circle. Nothing of what Paul accomplished could have happened without this body of co-workers. Finally, Paul's mission was fundamentally reliant on the Holy Spirit and his grace. If Paul had adopted a Bible verse as the motto for his mission, Zechariah 4:6 would have fit it to a tee: "Not by might, nor by power, but by my Spirit, says the LORD of hosts."

What I do not consider in this book is the heart of Paul's preaching, namely, the gospel, the glory of God in the face of the crucified and risen Christ. But doing justice to the apostle's preaching would require another book.

2 See especially his *The Ministry and Message of Paul* (Grand Rapids, MI: Zondervan Publishing House, 1971) and his *Paul, Apostle of Liberty: The Origin and Nature of Paul's Christianity*, 2nd ed. (Grand Rapids, MI; Cambridge, UK: William B. Eerdmans Publ. Co., 2015).

3 In his "Foreword" to the second edition of Longenecker's *Paul, Apostle of Liberty*, Douglas Campbell notes that Longenecker was "justly revered as much for his kindness as for his erudition" (*Paul, Apostle of Liberty*, xvi). For a beautiful tribute to Dr. Longenecker's scholarship, see James Ernest, "In Memoriam: Richard N. Longenecker, 1930–2021" (https://verbasparsa.org/2021/06/11/in-memoriam-richard-n-longenecker-1930-2021/; accessed March 25, 2022).

Acknowledgements

Books are odd things. Most of them have one person's name on the cover as author. But no one ever gets a book published without help. This one is no different, and I am grateful for advice and help received from these good friends: Matt Hall, Mike Pohlman, Stephen Wellum, Kirk Wellum and Don Whitney.

Dundas, Ontario
Easter Week, 2022

1

Conversion

By any standard, the apostle Paul lived an incredibly eventful life. He was transformed from a violent, pugilistic individual, prepared to kill for his religious beliefs, into a man of love, ever ready to die for his Saviour, Christ Jesus, who had died for him and loved him with an everlasting love. He survived assassination attempts, a number of shipwrecks, various stonings at the hands of mobs and corporal punishment meted out by Roman soldiers. He was the central driving force in the establishment of Christian communities around the shores of the Mediterranean, travelling some 25,000 kilometres during his ministry according to one estimate and planting a dozen or more churches.[1] And, of course, he penned thirteen books of the New Testament canon.

George Whitefield (1714–1770), the indefatigable evangelist of the eighteenth century, rightly asked of Paul: "Was he not filled with a holy, restless impatience and insatiable thirst of travelling, and undertaking dangerous voyages for the conversion of infidels?"[2] Adolf von Harnack (1851–1930), a remarkable historian though liberal in his theology, wrote this tribute about Paul:

---

[1] Eckhard J. Schnabel, *Paul the Missionary: Realities, Strategies and Methods* (Downers Grove, Illinois: InterVarsity Press; Nottingham: Apollos, 2008), 121–122.
[2] George Whitefield, *Some Remarks on a Pamphlet, Entitled, The Enthusiasm of Methodists and Papists Compar'd* (London: W. Strahan, 1749), 26.

What missionary is there, what preacher, what man entrusted
with the cure of souls, who can be compared with him,
whether in the greatness of the task which he accomplished
or in the holy energy with which he carried it out? He worked
with the most living of all messages, and kindled a fire; he
cared for his people like a father and strove for the souls of
others with all the forces of his own; at the same time he dis-
charged the duties of the teacher, the schoolmaster, the orga-
nizer. When he sealed his work by his death, the Roman
Empire from Antioch as far as Rome, nay, as far as Spain, was
planted with Christian communities.[3]

But how did Paul come to be such a missionary of Jesus? How
did he accomplish all that he did? What does all of this mean for
us today? This small book seeks to answer these questions by look-
ing at certain aspects of his mission: love as the motivating force
for his mission; his plans for a mission to Spain; the centrality of
prayer in Paul's mission; his co-workers; and finally, his reliance
on the Spirit of God. But first, we must begin with his conversion.

Paul before his conversion

Let me begin with the obvious: Paul was a Jew. He never lost sight
of the fact that as a member of the Jewish people, he was the recip-
ient of an incredible heritage. As he makes clear in Romans 9:4–5,
to the Israelites "belong the adoption, the glory, the covenants, the
giving of the law, the worship, and the promises…the patriarchs,
and from their race, according to the flesh, is the Christ who is God
over all, blessed forever." God had intended these gifts—the gift of
the covenants and the law, the Scriptures and the promise of the
Messiah—to be a means to help the rest of the world come to know
the living God, the God of Israel. However, the Jewish people had
by and large kept themselves separate from the nations, grown to
despise them and saw the one true God as only *their* God and not
the God of the Gentiles. In other words, the grace God had shown
Israel became a matter of ethnic pride.

---

[3] Adolf von Harnack, *What Is Christianity?* trans. Thomas Bailey Saunders, 2nd ed. rev.
(New York: G.P. Putnam's Sons; London: Williams and Norgate, 1908), 202–203.

In Philippians 3:4–6, we see very clearly some of the things in which Paul, before his conversion, took great pride. There was the fact that he was "circumcised on the eighth day, of the people of Israel, of the tribe of Benjamin" in his hometown of Tarsus (Acts 9:11; 21:29a).[4] Through the act of circumcision, which was established by God 2,000 years earlier as part of the covenant God made with Abraham, Paul was included among the people of God. Then, he was "a Hebrew of Hebrews." Most Jews outside Israel did not speak Hebrew, the ancient language of the people of God; they used Greek, the *lingua franca* of the eastern Mediterranean. Paul could speak Hebrew as if he had grown up in Israel.[5] As a young boy, probably when he was twelve or so, his family took him to study and live in Jerusalem with one of the most prominent rabbis of the day, Gamaliel, the son or grandson of Hillel. As Paul says in Acts 22:3:

I am a Jew, born in Tarsus in Cilicia, but brought up in this city, educated at the feet of Gamaliel according to the strict manner of the law of our fathers, being zealous for God as all of you are this day.[6]

Third, Paul was "as to the law, a Pharisee." He grew up in a very conservative Jewish family, demonstrated by his parents taking him to Jerusalem when he was twelve, as well as Paul's statement that he was "a Pharisee."[7] Also, Paul's family was probably a fairly well-to-do family of high social standing since they could afford to support him in Jerusalem as he studied.[8] Paul was so committed a Pharisee that he believed he was "blameless" in keeping the law (Philippians 3:6; see also Galatians 1:14: "I was advancing in Judaism

---

4 Schnabel, *Paul the Missionary*, 40–41; Paul Barnett, *Paul: Missionary of Jesus: After Jesus*, vol. 2 (Grand Rapids, MI; Cambridge, U.K.: William B. Eerdmans Publ. Co., 2008), 27–30. Paul also possessed Roman citizenship (Acts 22:28), which meant that his father must have been a citizen. It is interesting in this regard that Paul generally ministered in towns that were key centres of Roman power and influence.

5 Schnabel, *Paul the Missionary*, 41, sees this phrase as having a linguistic implication; Barnett, *Paul*, 33 disagrees and sees it as a further reference to a strict upbringing.

6 On Gamaliel, see Barnett, *Paul*, 34–36.

7 In Acts 23:6, Luke quotes Paul as saying, "I am a Pharisee, a son of Pharisees." See also Acts 22:3.

8 Schnabel, *Paul the Missionary*, 43.

beyond many of my own age among my people, so extremely zealous was I for the traditions of my fathers.") This is important. Paul did not seem to have wrestled with a guilty conscience prior to his conversion. As far as he was concerned, he was above reproach. It is also important to note that Paul would have been in Jerusalem during the ministry of Jesus, since he was formerly a contemporary of Christ. In Paul's eyes, the crucifixion of Christ would have meant that Christ was forsaken by God because of the well-known truism he states in Galatians 3:13: "Cursed is everyone who is hanged on a tree."

Finally, Paul was "as to zeal, a persecutor of the Church." In Galatians 1:13, Paul recalls how, in his former life in Judaism, he "persecuted the church of God violently and tried to destroy it." In 1 Timothy 1:13, he states that he was a "blasphemer, persecutor, and insolent opponent." That final word implied he had actually killed Christians. We know Paul was present at the death of Stephen, the first martyr. In Acts 8:1, we read that Paul "approved of his execution." Did Stephen's death give Paul remorse? There is no indication it did. Luke mentions Paul's presence to demonstrate the extent of his zeal for Pharisaism, not so much to indicate what might have been taking place within the mind and heart of the Pharisee Paul. In fact, it may well be the case that the killing of Stephen was the catalyst that launched Paul on his career as a persecutor.[9] For Paul, zeal for the law entailed an unconditional commitment to maintain Israel's distinctiveness. Paul was forceful and violent if necessary against both Gentiles and fellow Jews, whom he regarded as either apostates or not zealous enough.[10]

The conversion of Paul

Turning to Acts 9, we see that Paul's conversion is one of the most important events, if not the most important event, of the Book of Acts. How can we say this? Well, first of all, the story is recounted three times—in Acts 9, 22, 26—each time from a slightly different perspective. One of the issues uppermost in the mind of any ancient author was the size of the book or scroll he was writing.

---

9 Barnett, *Paul*, 45–53. See also Acts 22:20.
10 James D.G. Dunn, *The Theology of Paul the Apostle* (Grand Rapids, MI: William B. Eerdmans Publ. Co., 1998), 351–352.

The Book of Acts was at the maximum length for a scroll in the ancient world. If Luke did not consider the narrative of Paul's conversion tremendously important, he would never have taken up valuable space by recounting it no less than three times. In fact, it is noteworthy that the second account is somewhat longer than the first account and the third account is even longer than the second. Perhaps the significance of the event is meant to grow in the mind of the reader.[11]

Paul received letters from the high priest that gave him authority to arrest Christians, like Stephen, in Damascus and bring them to Jerusalem for trial. Damascus was an important commercial centre 135 miles northeast of Jerusalem. It had a considerable Jewish population, and as it lay on the main route from Egypt to Mesopotamia, it could easily become a key centre for the dissemination of the Christian message. On his way there, around midday, when the sun was its brightest, Paul saw a blazing light "brighter than the sun" (Acts 26:13). In the Old Testament, appearances of God were usually accompanied by a bright light.[12] In this case, Christ appeared—an implication of his deity.

The effect on Paul was so powerful that he lost his bodily strength and fell to the ground.[13] According to Acts 9:4–6 (similarly Acts 22:7–10), he then heard a voice. In Acts 26:14, Luke tells us the voice spoke in Hebrew: "Saul, Saul, why are you persecuting me?" Paul was confused by the question. He wasn't attacking God. In his mind, he had been serving God; it was the apostate Jewish followers of the accursed Jesus that he was rounding up for possible execution who were attacking God. Hence, he asked, "Who are you, Lord?" The term "Lord" (kyrios) is clearly a divine title. "I am Jesus, whom you are persecuting." As Jesus identified himself, one can only imagine what a traumatic shock it must have been for the Pharisee Saul. He now had the horrible realization that his zeal, instead of being approved of by God, had actually been against God.[14] Saul's

---

11 It is also good narrative technique to reserve some details for the later accounts.

12 See, for example, Isaiah 60:1–3, 19; Ezekiel 1:26–28; 10:1–4.

13 Many depictions of this aspect of Paul's conversion, show him falling from a horse. But there is no mention of a horse in the text.

14 The phrase in Acts 26:14, "It is hard for you to kick against the goads" is a Greek proverb. It depicts a goad, a wooden stick with metal spikes against which it was useless to kick since one would only hurt oneself. What is the meaning of the proverb in this

resulting "blindness was obviously due...to the sudden shock of being confronted with the glory of the one whom he thought of as a blasphemer."[15] This was not simply a *vision* of Jesus: Paul actually saw the risen Christ (1 Corinthians 15:8).

Is Paul converted at this point? No. But the experience on the road had begun a process that would surely result in a full conversion. Proof of that conversion was that he received the Spirit—see Acts 9:17—which is *the* proof of genuine conversion in the Book of Acts.[16] That day on the Damascus Road and the two days that followed saw the conversion of Paul from a persecutor of Christians and a man filled with hate and violence to a devoted follower of Christ and a lover of both Jew and Gentile. But there was more for Paul: there would be a call to be a missionary.

The calling of Paul as a missionary

Acts 9:10–19 recounts the way Ananias, a Christian disciple from Damascus,[17] had a vision and was told to go to "Straight Street," today Darb el-Mostakim. However, unlike Paul, Ananias knew who was speaking to him, as he said, "Here I am Lord" (verse 10). Despite some profound misgivings about the likelihood of real change in Paul, Ananias was obedient and went to see him. Thus, Ananias was there when Paul received the Spirit, which would have confirmed to Ananias the reality of Saul's conversion. It was probably Ananias who baptized Paul—though this is not explicitly stated. As found throughout Acts, baptism followed conversion.

Ananias also conveyed to Paul Christ's calling of him to be a missionary, as we read in Acts 9: 15–16: "Go, for he is a chosen instrument of mine to carry my name before the Gentiles and kings and the children of Israel. For I will show him how much he must suffer for the sake of my name." Acts 26:16–18 gives us a fuller version of the commissioning of Paul as a missionary

---

context? It emphasizes that it is ultimately "fruitless to struggle against God" (Ben Witherington, III, *The Acts of the Apostles: A Socio-Rhetorical Commentary* [Grand Rapids, MI; Cambridge, UK: William B. Eerdmans Publ. Co.; Carlisle, UK: Paternoster Press, 1998], 311). It does not refer to conviction of sin in Paul's conscience.

15 James D.G. Dunn, *Baptism in the Holy Spirit: A Re-examination of the New Testament Teaching on the Gift of the Spirit in Relation to Pentecostalism Today* (London: SCM Press, 1970), 75.

16 See the argument of Dunn, *Baptism in the Holy Spirit*.

17 Acts 22:12—"a devout man according to the law."

without any reference to Christ's intermediary Ananias. Luke cites the words of the risen Christ thus:

> I have appeared to you for this purpose, to appoint you as a servant and witness to the things in which you have seen me and to those in which I will appear to you, delivering you from your people and from the Gentiles—to whom I am sending you to open their eyes, so that they may turn from darkness to light and from the power of Satan to God, that they may receive forgiveness of sins and a place among those who are sanctified by faith in me.

Paul was being sent to the Gentiles to open their eyes so they would turn from "darkness to light." What does conversion entail according to this image? It means to come out of spiritual darkness into light.[18] Paul was being sent to the Gentiles so they might turn "from the power of Satan to God." In the final analysis, there are only two states: those who are living under the lordship of Christ and those who are under the power of Satan.[19] What is conversion, then? It is to be freed from the dominion of Satan to be a citizen of the kingdom of Christ. Finally, Paul was being sent to the Gentiles so they might "receive forgiveness of sins." What is conversion, then? It is to know that one's sins are forgiven, to have a place among the saints and to become a member of the church. The means by which all this takes place is faith in Christ. As Paul's call concludes, those who are members of the church are those who have been "sanctified," or set apart, "by faith in me."

Reflecting on Paul's conversion

Paul reflected on his own conversion a number of times in his letters. One of the most striking comes after those we have already been considering in Philippians 3. In Philippians 3:7–9, we read:

> But whatever gain I had, I counted as loss for the sake of Christ. Indeed, I count everything as loss because of the surpassing worth of knowing Christ Jesus my Lord. For his sake I have

---

18 See, in this regard, Colossians 1:12–13; 1 Peter 2:9; Ephesians 5:8.
19 See Ephesians 2:1–2; 1 Thessalonians 1:9; 1 John 5:19.

suffered the loss of all things and count them as rubbish, in
order that I may gain Christ and be found in him, not having
a righteousness of my own that comes from the law, but that
which comes through faith in Christ, the righteousness from
God that depends on faith.

This is true Christianity: finding favour with God through Christ
and Christ alone. It is not through one's keeping of a set of rules or
being faithful to a certain way or tradition of being religious—
whether Jewish or Catholic or Muslim, or Reformed or Brethren
or Baptist. The heart of Paul's missionality or missions-minded-
ness is that Christianity is a *chosen faith* not an *inherited religion*. In
the words of the African theologian Tertullian (*fl.* AD 190–220), it
is natural for a person "to become a Christian, not to be born one
(*fieri enim, non nasci solet Christiana*)."[20]

Paul realized he was wrong to believe that violence and force can
promote the kingdom of God. He also came to understand that
salvation cannot be based on one's doings, one's works, no matter
how good they might appear. In truth, these works are all stained
with degrees of sin. Thus, Paul became a lover of Christ. Christ, in
his death, took all of Paul's sins upon himself and gave him the
flawless holiness that marked Jesus' earthly life and ministry.[21]

Four centuries later, the North African theologian Augustine
(AD 354–430) would breathe the same spirit as Paul. He wrote
about his conversion, which came about through reading a passage
from Paul's letter to the Romans:

During all those years [of rebellion], where was my free will?
What was the hidden, secret place from which it was sum-
moned in a moment, so that I might bend my neck to your
easy yoke …? How sweet all at once it was for me to be rid of
those fruitless joys which I had once feared to lose…! You
drove them from me, you who are the true, the sovereign
joy. You drove them from me and took their place, you who
are sweeter than all pleasure…you who outshine all light…

---

20 Tertullian, *On the Testimony of the Soul* 1.7. The author's translation. This text can be
found at https://www.tertullian.org/latin/testimonio.htm; accessed April 9, 2022.
21 See 2 Corinthians 5:21.

you who surpass all honor...O Lord my God, my Light, my Wealth, and my Salvation.[22]

This kind of conversion does not happen only to extraordinary theologians and pastors like Paul and Augustine. A farmer's wife, the Welsh hymnwriter Ann Griffiths (1776–1805), shared the same kind of conversion. She writes poignantly about her experience:

> Gladly would I leave behind me
> All the idols I have known,
> Since I bear inscribed the likeness
> Of a more exalted One;
> Worthy of unending worship,
> Love, and reverence is he;
> By his precious death were myriads
> From the jaws of death set free.

Or listen to these other words that Ann penned:

> Let my days be wholly given
> Jesus' blood to glorify,
> Calm to rest beneath his shadow,
> At his feet to live and die,
> Love the cross, and bear it daily,
> ('Tis the cross my Husband bore,)
> Gaze with joy upon his Person,
> And unceasingly adore.[23]

This is conversion. Such experiences lay at the heart of the Pauline mission.

---

[22] Cited John Piper, "The Swan Is Not Silent: Sovereign Joy in the Life and Thought of St. Augustine" (Talk at the Bethlehem Conference for Pastors, 1998).

[23] See A.M. Allchin, *Songs to Her God: Spirituality of Ann Griffiths* (Cambridge, MA: Cowley Publications, 1987), 104, 113.

STUDY GUIDE | *Application & reflection*

1. This chapter outlines the things Paul took pride in before his conversion, which he thought put him in good standing before God. If you are converted, are there any things you relied on for your standing with God before your conversion?

2. Read Acts 9. What stands out to you about Paul's experience? Why?

3. What is true conversion? Describe in your own words.

4. Paul was called to be a missionary to the Gentiles at the time of his conversion, as this chapter explains. Why is this significant? What challenges come to mind as you consider Paul's "former way of life" as a persecutor of the church?

5. Read Philippians 3:7–9 where Paul reflects on his conversion. What is Paul's central point in this passage?

6. Conversion is foundational to Paul's mission. Have you been converted? If not, what are some things holding you back? If so, what do you see as *your* mission?

2

Love

Among the most precious texts of God's Word is Ephesians 5:25b: "Christ…loved the church and gave himself for her." Before time began or space was formed, the One we know as the Lord Jesus Christ had set his heart on dying for human sinners. Christ came into this world to die for the church, not out of necessity nor from need, not by constraint nor grudgingly, but from a heart of love, out of mercy and kindness, freely and willingly.

Equally, the Holy Spirit, whom Christ gave in his stead when he ascended to the right hand of the Father, also loves the church for which Christ died. After all, it is the Holy Spirit who laid the church's apostolic foundation on the day of Pentecost.[1] It is the Spirit who adds men and women to the church as he enables them to confess Christ as Lord.[2] It is the Spirit who pours the love of God into their hearts, draws them to worship God and to pray to him as "Dear Father."[3] It is the Spirit who lavishes gifts on the church so she might grow in spiritual maturity and bring glory to the One who is ever at the centre of all the Spirit's work, namely, the Lord Jesus.[4]

It properly follows that one of the marks of being filled with the Spirit is participation in this love of the Spirit for the church.[5]

---

[1] Acts 2. See also Ephesians 2:19–22; 3:5.
[2] 1 Corinthians 12:3.
[3] Romans 5:5; Philippians 3:3; Galatians 4:6.
[4] 1 Corinthians 12; Ephesians 4:11–13; John 16:14.
[5] 1 John 3:16–24.

Those who are led by the Spirit, those who are filled with the Spirit, love the people of God.

"The love of the Spirit"

The Spirit's creation of love for the people of God appears in Romans 15. Paul was about to embark on a dangerous trip to Judaea and Jerusalem where he knew he would face "unbelievers" who were strong opponents of the gospel.[6] So Paul requested his readers in Rome to remember to pray for him. Adding to the solemnity of this appeal for prayer is the two-fold basis on which the apostle makes his request. First, the admonition Paul gives to his readers is "through our Lord Jesus Christ." Here Paul invokes the authority of the one Lord, to whom both he and his readers are bound as servants.[7] He says, in effect, because Christ is their Lord, they ought to pray for his servant who is seeking the advance of his Master's kingdom and the exaltation of his dear name.[8]

Secondly, he makes this request "by the love of the Spirit." This is a unique phrase in the Scriptures. Elsewhere when the Scriptures speak of the love of one of the divine persons, it is always the love of the Father or the love of Christ.[9] Moreover, it is not immediately clear what Paul means by the phrase:

1. Is it the love that believers have for the Holy Spirit?
2. Is it the love that the Spirit has for believers?
3. Is it the love that the Holy Spirit produces in believers for one another?

Few commentators think that the first option is a possibility here. The second option was held by, among others, John Ryland, Jr.

---

6 Romans 15:30–31.

7 C.E.B. Cranfield, *A Critical and Exegetical Commentary on the Epistle to the Romans* (1979 ed.; repr. Edinburgh: T. & T. Clark, 1986), II, 776.

8 See Chapter 4 for a deeper discussion of the prayer in this passage.

9 Gordon D. Fee, *God's Empowering Presence: The Holy Spirit in the Letters of Paul* (Peabody, MA: Hendrickson Publishers, 1994), 632. For an exposition of the love of the Spirit for the believer that draws on a variety of biblical texts about the Spirit's work, see Robert Philip, *The Love of the Spirit Traced in His Work* (1836 ed.; repr. Grand Rapids, MI: Reformation Heritage Books, 2006).

(1753–1825), the close friend of William Carey (1761–1834),[10] and John Murray (1898–1975), the Presbyterian theologian who taught at Westminster Theological Seminary for much of his life and wrote a superb commentary on Romans.[11] The interpretation of John Calvin (1509–1564), though, is the one that probably makes the best sense here. He interprets the phrase as the love "by which the saints ought to embrace one another."[12] As Calvin goes on to say: "The love of the Spirit means the love by which Christ joins us together, because it is not of the flesh, nor of the world, but proceeds from his Spirit who is the bond of our unity."[13] In this reading of the phrase, Paul is basing his appeal on the fact that his readers are indwelt by the Spirit and as such know something of the love that the Spirit produces in believers for one another. Paul thus expects that those who love God's people will pray for them. To paraphrase the apostle John: the one who says he loves God's people and never prays for them is a liar.

"Constrained by the Spirit"

Now, this trip to Jerusalem is also treated at some length by Luke in the final section of the Book of Acts. On the way to Jerusalem, Paul, with his apostolic band and a few other brothers,[14] stopped at Miletus where he asked the elders in Ephesus to come and meet him. As Paul met with the Ephesian elders, he told them that he was "constrained by the Spirit" to go up to Jerusalem. Although the Spirit had been bearing witness through various Christian prophets that he would face "imprisonment and afflictions,"[15] he was not certain what awaited him there. Luke tells us that a little further on in the journey, Paul and his apostolic band reached the ancient Phoenician city of Tyre. There, during a meeting, some of

---

10 John Ryland, "The Love of the Spirit" in his *Pastoral Memorials: Selected from the Manuscripts of the Late Revd. John Ryland, D.D. of Bristol* (London: B.J. Holdsworth, 1828), II, 42–43.

11 John Murray, *The Epistle to the Romans* (Grand Rapids, MI: Wm. B. Eerdmans Publ. Co., 1965), 221.

12 John Calvin, *The Epistles of Paul the Apostle to the Romans and to the Thessalonians*, trans. Ross Mackenzie (1960 ed., repr.; Grand Rapids, MI: Wm. B. Eerdmans Publ. Co., 1973), 317. See also Fee, *God's Empowering Presence*, 633.

13 Calvin, *Epistles of Paul the Apostle to the Romans and to the Thessalonians*, 317.

14 For a list of some of those accompanying Paul, see Acts 20:4.

15 Acts 20:22–23.

the brothers urged the apostle—"through the Spirit"—not to go to Jerusalem.[16]

At Caesarea, yet another stop on the journey, Paul and his co-workers lodged with Philip the evangelist. While there, Paul was again warned, this time by the prophet Agabus, what awaited him at Jerusalem. "Thus says the Holy Spirit," Agabus solemnly announced as he took Paul's belt and bound his own hands and feet. "This is how the Jews will bind the man who owns this belt and deliver him into the hands of the Gentiles." This prophecy was too much for Paul's companions who now pled with him not to continue the journey. But Paul, knowing that the Spirit was leading him up to Jerusalem, was determined to go on. He was ready, as he told his friends and the brothers in Caesarea, "not only to be imprisoned but even to die in Jerusalem for the name of the Lord Jesus."[17]

So, the Spirit led Paul up to Jerusalem, where he did indeed experience afflictions and imprisonment at the hands of the Romans.[18] But—and this is vital to answer—why did the Spirit lead him to Jerusalem? In short, the answer can be put this way: it was because of the Spirit's love for the church, and especially his delight in the unity of believers in Christ.

The collection and the Spirit[19]
Go back to Romans 15. Here we find the reason Paul took this dangerous trip to Jerusalem in the first place. There Paul informed the Roman believers he was coming to Rome and he intended to go from there to Spain. But before he headed to Rome he first had to go up to Jerusalem.[20] As he writes in verses 25–28:

> At present, I am going to Jerusalem to bringing aid to the saints. For Macedonia and Achaia have been pleased to make some contribution for the poor among the saints at Jerusalem.

16 Acts 21:4.
17 Acts 21:13.
18 See Acts 21:27–28:31.
19 For the following section of this chapter, I am drawing on my earlier studies: "The Collection for the Saints," *Reformation Today* 158 (July/Aug 1997): 7–10; and "Paul: Collecting Money and Maintaining the Unity of the Spirit," *The Banner of Truth* 541 (October 2008): 15–23.
20 Romans 15:23–24.

They were pleased to do it, and indeed they owe it to them. For if the Gentiles have come to share in their spiritual blessings, they ought also to be of service to them in material blessings. When therefore, I have completed this and have delivered to them what has been collected, I will leave for Spain by way of you.

Paul was going up to Jerusalem to deliver a collection of money for the poor believers there. Who were these poor saints and how did they come to be poor? What were the historical circumstances that prompted Paul to begin making such a collection in the first place?

To answer these questions, we have to go back to the earliest days of the Jerusalem church. Soon after Pentecost, this first Christian community exuberantly sold their real estate and their personal possessions, "had all things in common," and sought to ensure that there were no poor among them.[21] In doing this, these believers were not seeking to obey any explicit commandment from Christ. Rather, their motivation was a simple desire to make it plain for all to see that in Christ they had "one heart and one soul."[22]

By disposing of their financial reserves in this way, however, the community placed itself in a highly vulnerable position. Persecution would aggravate this situation.[23] Moreover, during the AD 40s there were a series of food shortages in Palestine and a particularly severe famine in AD 48 that appeared to have triggered a financial crisis in the Jerusalem church.[24] Thus, when the apostle Paul went up to Jerusalem in the very year this famine struck, he was specifically asked by the leaders there to "remember the poor."[25] In making this suggestion, the leaders of the Jerusalem church did not know that this reminder would become a major part of Paul's life and ministry for nearly a decade. Scott McKnight goes so far

---

21 Acts 2:44–45; 4:32–35.
22 Acts 4:32; Max Scheler, *Ressentiment*, ed. L.A. Coser and trans. W.W. Holdheim (New York: Schocken Books, 1972), 111–112.
23 Compare the persecution described in Hebrews 10:33–34, where the loss of material possessions and goods was involved.
24 Keith F. Nickle, *The Collection: A Study in Paul's Strategy* (Napierville, IL.: Alec R. Allenson, 1966), 24, 29–32; S. McKnight, "Collection for the Saints" in *Dictionary of Paul and His Letters*, ed. Gerald F. Hawthorne and Ralph P. Martin, with Daniel G. Reid (Downers Grove, IL/Leicester: InterVarsity Press, 1993), 144.
25 Galatians 2:10.

as to describe it as "Paul's obsession for nearly two decades."[26] While this may be something of an exaggeration, caring for the poor was of great importance to the apostle.

This collection involved elaborate plans to gather a substantial amount of money from the various churches Paul had planted among the Gentiles.[27] Once the money had been gathered, it was to be delivered to the Jewish believers in Jerusalem to help provide succour and aid for the poorest of them. Paul came to see this collection as a marvelous opportunity to demonstrate to the Jerusalem church—and believers everywhere—that even as there was one Lord and one gospel, so also there was *one people* of God.[28]

In Romans 15:27, Paul indicates succinctly his view of the collection: it was nothing less than a concrete and visible expression of the unity Jewish and Gentile believers had in Christ. Paul and other missionaries to the Gentiles had been sent out by the Jewish believers in Palestine to bring the light of the gospel to those imprisoned in the dark dungeon of paganism. As a result, the Gentiles had become partakers in the *spiritual* blessings of the Jewish Christians. Through this witness of Jewish believers, these Gentiles had been taught the things of the Spirit. Having such unity in spiritual things, it was only proper that the Gentiles minister to their Jewish brothers and sisters in *material* things. In fact, the word Paul uses in Romans 15:26 to describe the collection is *koinonia*, which in other contexts in Paul's writings is translated "fellowship." The sharing by Gentile believers of their financial resources with their brothers and sisters in Palestine was not simply a gift of money and nothing more. For Paul it speaks of their common life in Christ and, as such, it is a sign of fellowship and proof of their love for the brethren.[29]

Paul's last word on the collection in Romans 15 is noteworthy. Paul gave no indication he thought this substantial gift of money would solve *all* the financial hardship and problems of the Jerusalem believers. But he hoped and prayed it would convince

---

26 McKnight, "Collection for the Saints," 143.
27 See 1 Corinthians 16:1–4; 2 Corinthians 8–9. The reference in 2 Corinthians 8:20 to this collection being a "lavish gift" points to the substantial amount of money involved.
28 McKnight, "Collection for the Saints," 145.
29 James D.G. Dunn, *Romans 9–16*, Word Biblical Commentary, vol.38B (Dallas, TX: Word Publishing, 1988), 875.

the believers in Jerusalem that just as there is one gospel and one Lord, so there is one people of God, bound together by one Spirit and demonstrating that unity in real, tangible ways. For Paul, the collection had become far more than a gift to relieve poverty and physical suffering. It was a powerful symbol of the unity of God's people in the Spirit, a unity that had been brought into being by a Spirit-empowered embrace of the gospel. The one gospel preached to different ethnic groups had produced one people of God.

As has been pointed out, in taking this collection to Jerusalem Paul was well aware of the dangers he faced. Thus, he asked the Roman Christians to pray fervently that his "service for Jerusalem" would be "acceptable to the saints."[30] Paul's sense of the dangers that awaited him in Jerusalem was not unfounded. After he had delivered the collection to the believers there,[31] the presence of one of his Gentile brothers with him caused him trouble. Seen in the Temple by Jewish zealots who hated both him and the gospel he preached, he was wrongly accused of defiling the Temple by bringing one of the Gentiles, the Ephesian Trophimus, into those areas of the Temple reserved for the Jews.[32] A mob wanted to kill the apostle, and he was rescued only at the last moment by the Romans. Placed under arrest, he spent the next four years as a Roman prisoner. It was in chains that he finally arrived in Rome.

"The unity of the Spirit"

One of the apostle Paul's deepest convictions was that the death of the Lord Jesus had not only reconciled God and those for whom Christ died but it had also broken down the barriers that divide men and women from one another. This conviction first comes to expression in Galatians, where Paul asserts that in Christ Jesus "there is neither Jew nor Greek, there is neither slave nor free, there is neither male nor female."[33] In the presence of God, all men and women are on an equal footing: all are sinners and all need to come to God the same way, through faith alone in the Lord Jesus Christ alone. In the context of this letter, this verse is a

---

30 Romans 15:31.
31 See Acts 24:17 for the sole reference to the actual collection in Acts.
32 Acts 21:27–29. Trophimus had come up with Paul to Jerusalem as a representative of the churches in Asia. For the other representatives, see Acts 20:4.
33 Galatians 3:28.

sharp rebuke to those individuals who were troubling the Galatian believers by urging them to believe that for salvation one had to embrace all the distinctive features of Judaism. Paul strongly disagreed. Religious background, race, even gender, are meaningless issues when one stands in God's holy presence. There only one thing matters: Does Christ Jesus know you as his own? One's religious heritage, one's economic standing, one's gender—all fade away in the light of one's answer to that most important of all questions, "Do you know God through his Son, the Lord Jesus Christ?

A few years later, some Corinthian believers, "restless experientialists,"[34] became overly impressed with one of the more spectacular spiritual gifts, namely, speaking in tongues. They were in danger of despising those who did not manifest this gift. Paul was quick to remind them that every believer in the body of Christ was a gifted individual whom the body needed to function properly.[35] "In one Spirit," he declared, all believers were "baptized into one body—Jews or Greeks, slaves or free—and all were made to drink of one Spirit."[36] The fundamental unity of Christians, established by the Holy Spirit on the basis of the death of Christ, is a unity that transcends religious heritage, economic status, and in this context, even spiritual giftedness.

In Romans, Paul again returns to an issue he had taken up in his letter to the Galatians: How do sinful men and women find complete and full acceptance by a holy and just God? Some Jewish Christians found it extremely difficult to shed the basic assumptions with which they had grown up. They maintained that their Jewish religious heritage, epitomized in circumcision and strict adherence to the Jewish food laws, was necessary for salvation. We see this struggle in the life of the apostle Peter over wrestling with whether it was right to eat with Gentile believers.[37]

Paul's response to this struggle is twofold. First, he systematically laid out, for his own day and for all time, the only way that a

---

34 This apt description is that of J.I. Packer, *A Quest for Godliness: The Puritan Vision of the Christian Life* (Wheaton, IL: Crossway Books, 1990), 30.

35 See 1 Corinthians 12–14.

36 1 Corinthians 12:13.

37 See Galatians 2:11–13.

man or a woman finds peace with God: since "all," both Jew and
Gentile, "have sinned and fall short of the glory of God,"[38] then all
must come to God in the identical way, namely, through faith in
Christ Jesus, who was crucified for sinners. As Paul says later in
the tenth chapter of Romans: "there is no distinction between Jew
and Greek; the same Lord is Lord of all, bestowing his riches on
all who call on him. For 'everyone who calls on the name of the
Lord will be saved.'"[39]

Paul was willing to give his life for the sake of this unity created
by the Spirit and take up to Jerusalem a tangible witness to that
unity: a collection of money from Gentile Christian pockets for
the relief of poor Jewish believers. When Paul later wrote from a
prison cell in Rome to the Ephesian church that they needed to
be zealous to preserve the "unity of the Spirit," the apostle knew
from real experience something of what this might cost.[40]
Centuries later, John Calvin echoed the heart of Paul's thinking
when, in his preface to his commentary on 2 Thessalonians, he
said, "My ministry...ought to be dearer to me than my own life."[41]
Like Paul, he knew that all who love what the Spirit loves can
walk no other path.

If one compares this Paul, willing to die for the Spirit's work in
unifying believers, to the Saul, whom the risen Christ transformed
on the Damascus Road, what a change there had been in temper
and passion! That Saul had been a religious zealot filled with hate
and violence for the followers of the Lord Jesus. This Paul was
now a man of love, willing to be killed for the sake of Christ and
his work through the Spirit in the church.

Why the change? The Spirit who had come to indwell him was
none other than the Spirit of love and the Spirit of unity. Thus it is
with all men and women who are truly Spirit-filled; they are men
and women of love, an essential in the Pauline mission. As Paul

---

[38] Romans 3:23.
[39] Romans 10:12–13.
[40] Ephesians 4:3.
[41] John Calvin, "To that distinguished man Benedict Textor, Physician" in his *Epistles
of Paul the Apostle to the Romans and to the Thessalonians*, 385. I am indebted for this
reference to Victor Shepherd, "My Ministry Is Dearer to Me than Life" (Sermon,
Annual Meeting of the Centre for Mentorship and Theological Reflection, Toronto, at
Tyndale Seminary, Toronto, June 5, 2008).

wrote many years later in 1 Timothy 1:5, the ultimate goal (*telos*) of his ministry was love that came "from a pure heart and a good conscience and a sincere faith."

STUDY GUIDE | *Application & reflection*

1. Read Ephesians 5:25. According to this chapter, "Those who are led by the Spirit, those who are filled with the Spirit, love the people of God." What does love for God's people look like in a practical way?

2. Paul sees prayer for one another as one of the most important ways we show our love for the people of God. What is necessary for us to pray for one another? What hinders this type of prayer?

3. Paul speaks of being "constrained by the Spirit" (Acts 20:22). What does this mean?

4. The churches in Macedonia and Achaea had set aside a "collection" for the poor among the saints in Jerusalem (Romans 15:25–28). Why were these people poor? What prompted Paul to make a collection for them?

5. What did Paul hope this collection would do for the saints in Jerusalem?

6. Why is giving and making "collections" for God's people important for Christians today?

7. What does "unity in the Spirit" mean? What does it not mean?

8. What hinders this unity today?

9. How does Paul say someone finds "peace with God"?

3

Mission

Historically evangelicals have been a people of mission, filled with a prayerful and active concern for the salvation of the lost. It is part of the warp and woof of being an evangelical. Reflect on these three examples—all from the Evangelical Baptist tradition. First, that quintessential nineteenth-century Baptist, C.H. Spurgeon (1834–1892), who, at the age of twenty-five and not long after he had been called to be the pastor of the Metropolitan Tabernacle, solemnly resolved: "God sparing my life, if I have my people at my back I will not rest until the dark county of Surrey [which lay to the south of London, where his church was located] be covered with places of worship."[1] In the providence of God, Spurgeon was involved in the planting of some seventy to eighty churches in London and the surrounding area.

Andrew Fuller (1754–1815), whom Spurgeon regarded as the leading theologian among British Calvinistic Baptists in the late eighteenth and early nineteenth centuries, echoed a similar sentiment when he declared that the "true churches of Jesus Christ travail in birth for the salvation of men. They are the armies of the Lamb, the grand object of whose existence is to extend the Redeemer's kingdom."[2] Fuller was, of course, the theological

---

[1] Cited Mike Nicholls, *C.H. Spurgeon: The Pastor Evangelist* (London: The Baptist Historical Society, 1992), 97.

[2] Andrew Fuller, *The Promise of the Spirit, the Grand Encouragement in Promoting the Gospel* in *The Complete Works of the Rev. Andrew Fuller* (1845 ed.; repr. Harrisonburg, VA: Sprinkle Publications, 1988), III, 359.

mainspring behind the launching of the Baptist Missionary Society that sent out as its first missionary William Carey (1761–1834), Fuller's close friend.

Finally, the seventeenth-century Puritan John Bunyan (1628–1688), who both Spurgeon and Fuller deeply admired, once said that the "great desire" of his heart was

> to get into the darkest places in the country, even amongst those people that were furthest off of profession; yet not because I could not endure the light (for I feared not to shew my Gospel to any) but because I found my spirit learned most after awakening and converting work, and the Word that I carried did lean itself most that way; Yea, so have I strived to preach the Gospel, not where Christ was named, lest I should build upon another man's foundation, Rom. 15.20. In my preaching I have really been in pain, and have as it were travailed to bring forth children to God; neither could I be satisfied unless some fruits did appear in my work: if I were fruitless it mattered not who commended me; but if I were fruitful, I cared not who did condemn.[3]

What helped to fuel these three men's zeal for the salvation of lost men and women was the example of early Christians like the apostle Paul. Bunyan, in fact, explicitly cites a verse in which the apostle's passion for evangelism is most evident—Romans 15:20: "Yea, so have I strived to preach the gospel, not where Christ was named, lest I should build upon another man's foundation." This verse is part of a somewhat larger passage, Romans 15:18–24, the one we have been considering in the previous chapter and which is found in the middle of Paul's concluding remarks. It is his most systematic exposition of the nature of the gospel as it relates to doctrine and lifestyle. It offers a very important window of understanding into Paul's thinking about his calling as an apostle.

At the very outset of his letter to the Romans, Paul had told the believers in Rome of his hopes to come to see them, to encourage

---

3 John Bunyan, *Grace Abounding to the Chief of Sinners*, 289–290, ed. W.R. Owens, *John Bunyan: Grace Abounding to the Chief of Sinners* (Harmondsworth, Middlesex: Penguin Books Ltd., 1987), 72–73, altered.

them, to strengthen them through the preaching of the gospel and to be encouraged by them in return (1:10–15). At the end of his letter in Romans 15:14–24, he comes back to these travel plans. Here, Paul emphasizes four things. First, there is an overwhelming sense of God's unmerited favour, his grace and mercy, which lay at the foundation of his entire mission and ministry to the Gentiles (verse 15). Then, there is God's grace at work in the past as he tells his readers about the shape of his ministry up to that point in time and its location, the main area of the Mediterranean. Third, there is grace expected for the future as he goes on to inform the Roman believers of his plans to visit them in Rome and his hope that he will be able to move on from there to Spain, the western extremity of the Roman Empire. Finally, this passage clearly reveals the heart of the apostle's ministry: the glorification of God in the establishment of local churches.

Paul's missionary labours in the eastern Mediterranean

Paul was quite conscious that he was called to be a pioneer evangelist and a builder of foundations. As mentioned in the first chapter, at his commissioning as an apostle, he had been explicitly told by the risen Christ that he was being sent to the Gentiles "to open their eyes, in order to turn them from darkness to light, and from the power of Satan to God" (Acts 26:18). Over the next twenty years, Paul unashamedly proclaimed the gospel in many strongholds of Satan. He went to Corinth, such a sinkhole of iniquity that the phrase "to live like a Corinthian" was synonymous with someone living a promiscuous and immoral lifestyle. Paul visited Ephesus, the site of the idolatrous Temple of Artemis, one of the seven wonders of the ancient world. He went to Athens as well, the centre of many of the great pride-inducing intellectual systems of the Graeco-Roman world.

But while Paul preached and taught, the invincible power of the Holy Spirit accompanied his preaching (Romans 15:19). Numerous Gentiles were drawn by that sovereign power out of the darkness of spiritual death and freed from their bondage to sin. They were brought into the light of God's kingdom and joined to other believers in local churches, delivered from the clutches of Satan and made alive to God. Paul's mission, in the providence of

God, was absolutely vital to the establishment of Christianity in the Roman world. Proof of this can be found in the large portion of the Book of Acts devoted to his ministry. Luke, its author, tells the story of Paul's conversion no less than three times. The significance of Paul's mission is also found in the fact that 13 of the books of the New Testament were written by him.

Paul consciously made his aim clear. He tells us in Romans 15:20, "from Jerusalem all the way around to [*mechri*] Illyricum, I have fully proclaimed the gospel of Christ" (NIV). His goal was to proclaim the gospel in cities and towns where the glorious name of Jesus Christ had never been named in worship, and never acknowledged and confessed as Lord. By the grace of God, churches were founded in key centres and major cities from Jerusalem all the way round to the region of Illyricum, which ran down the eastern coast of the Adriatic Gulf (Romans 15:15,19).[4] Paul thus tells us that his ministry had been focused on the northeastern quadrant of the Mediterranean. In speaking of this area, Paul aptly used the term *kyklo*—literally "in a circle," that is, "in a sweep around." Paul sees the line from Jerusalem to Illyricum[5] as the radius of a circle. Paul was specifically led by the Spirit of God to target this geographical area as the locality of his early ministry.

Neither Paul's writings or the Book of Acts indicate that he ever considered exercising a ministry as a church-planter in Egypt, in other parts of the southern Mediterranean coast or toward peoples outside of the Roman Empire, such as the Parthians to the east of the Empire or the Germanic tribes to the north.[6] Obviously, Paul left it to other pioneer evangelists to take the gospel to these regions. What he knew was God had called him to evangelize this particular region on the northern coast of the Mediterranean.

It is significant that Paul describes his ministry in Romans 15:20 as one of laying foundations. This was an image he had also used in 1 Corinthians 3:10 when he thought about the exact shape of his life's work. There he writes to inform his readers that it was

---

4 Today, this area is Albania and what was once Yugoslavia.
5 When Paul preached in Illyricum is not known. The term *mechri* can mean "up to," that is "up to the border of" Illyricum.
6 W.P. Bowers, "Mission" in Gerald F. Hawthorne, Ralph P. Martin and Daniel G. Reid, eds., *Dictionary of Paul and His Letters* (Downers Grove, IL; Leicester: InterVarsity Press, 1993), 612.

as a "wise master builder" that he had laid "the foundation" of the church in Corinth. It is hardly accidental that in describing his ministry, Paul does not write of simply making bricks, that is, winning individual Gentiles to Christ. Rather, Paul pictures himself in both of these verses as a builder of "buildings," that is, a founder of *communities* that are Christ-centred in their worship, their doctrine and their life.[7]

His goal as a pioneer evangelist and missionary was not only the saving of the lost, but also the gathering together of those who had been converted into communities of like-minded men and women. P.T. O'Brien writes that for Paul "conversion to Christ means incorporation into him, and thus membership within a Christian community."[8] In fact, as O'Brien goes on to note, Paul sees such communities as proof of the reality of his calling. Paul would surely have appreciated the insight of John Wesley (1703–1791), the founder of Methodism, that Christianity was never meant to be a solitary religion. Paul would have considered it very odd if Christians were not committed to a local church as members. Paul believed that we have been saved to be part of a local church, a manifestation of that universal body of believers.

Is this your vision of evangelism as a believer? It should not simply be the conversion of individuals, but the building of a Christian community where new believers can be nurtured on the Word of God and grow into Christian maturity. There they can regularly partake of the Lord's Supper, that ordinance which so powerfully speaks of the corporate unity of believers in Christ. There they can know the joys of Christian fellowship.

Paul's plans for ministry in the western Mediterranean

It was ministry in the northeastern quadrant of the Mediterranean that had prevented Paul from travelling to Rome before the writing of this letter (Romans 15:22), but he came to the conviction that his pioneer ministry in that area was drawing to a close. How he knew this we are not told. Such a sense of direction has been given

---

[7] Bowers, "Mission," 609.

[8] P.T. O'Brien, *Gospel and Mission in the Writings of Paul: An Exegetical and Theological Analysis* (Grand Rapids, MI: Baker; Carlisle, UK: Paternoster Press, 1995), 42.

to other servants of God down through the years. For instance, when Martyn Lloyd-Jones (1899–1981) came to retire in 1968 from his marvellous ministry at Westminster Chapel in London, he did so with a deep conviction that one phase of his ministry was being brought to an end and another was about to begin. He had undergone a serious operation for cancer that year. He later wrote that this was only "a precipitating factor in what was becoming an increasing conviction." When he discovered that he needed this operation, he said: "I felt that God was saying to me, 'This is the end of one ministry and the beginning of another.'"[9] We do not know what factors God brought into Paul's life to convince the apostle that he "no longer had a place in these parts" (Romans 15:23). The conviction appears to have been similar to that of Lloyd-Jones: God was bringing to an end one phase of his missionary work and launching him out into another.

As to the locality of the new ministry Paul believed God was giving him, it was Spain, at the other end of the Mediterranean.[10] Whether or not the apostle ever set foot on Spanish soil is a matter of some debate among the commentators. The sixteenth-century Reformer John Calvin felt that it is quite uncertain whether Paul reached Spain.[11] However, Thomas Scott (1747–1821), the evangelical Anglican commentator of the early nineteenth century, believed Paul did. In support of his view, Scott cited the early Christian document known as *1 Clement*. This early Christian writing was written by an elder in the church at Rome toward the end of the first century. This letter stated that Paul journeyed as far as "the limits of the west," that is, to Spain.[12]

---

9 D. Martyn Lloyd-Jones, *Letters 1991–1981*, selected Iain H. Murray (Edinburgh: The Banner of Truth Trust, 1994), 214.

10 It is noteworthy that Paul's ministry is still focused on the northern Mediterranean. James D.G. Dunn thus thinks it quite probable that "Paul's grand design was to cover the northern half of the Mediterranean while others covered the southern half" (*Romans 9–16*, Word Biblical Commentary, vol. 38B [1988 ed.; repr. Milton Keynes: Word (UK) Ltd., 1991], 872).

11 John Calvin, *The Epistles of Paul the Apostle to the Romans and to the Thessalonians*, trans. Ross Mackenzie (1960 ed.; repr. Grand Rapids, MI: Wm. B. Eerdmans Publ. Co., 1973), 314.

12 Thomas Scott, *The Holy Bible* (Boston: Crocker and Brewster, 1858), VI, 107. On the phrase "the limits of the west" as a reference to Spain or possibly Gaul, see E. Earle Ellis, "'The End of the Earth' (Acts 1:8)," *Bulletin for Biblical Research* 1 (1991): 129.

It is profitable and instructive to look at the challenges which Paul must have reflected on as he contemplated this new missionary undertaking. The Romans had begun the conquest of Spain in the third century BC and by Paul's day the country was firmly under Roman rule. There were two major difficulties he would have had to face in seeking to evangelize Spain.

Two problems

The first problem was that until the third and fourth centuries AD, there was no evidence at all of any substantial Jewish settlements or synagogues in Spain.[13] Paul's usual missionary strategy in the eastern Mediterranean had been to make the synagogue the *initial* place of evangelism when he came to establish a local church in a city. For example, when he went to Athens, he first went to the synagogue to reason about Christ with the Jews and Gentile worshippers (Acts 17:16–17). Invariably, Paul would run into opposition in the synagogue, and eventually he would have to find another venue for evangelism. It is clear from Acts that the synagogue was the first place that Paul would seek to win a hearing for the gospel. This is quite understandable since Jesus, as the Messiah, fulfils all of the prophecies predicted about him throughout the Old Testament. Paul and those who attended the synagogue reverenced the Old Testament Scriptures as a pure revelation from God, something Greek and Roman pagans certainly did not. If there were no significant Jewish settlements in Spain, this method of evangelism would need to be changed. Paul had to have expected to begin his evangelistic ministry in totally pagan surroundings, where there was no devotion to the Old Testament and where there would be little, if any, initial interest in a proclamation that Jesus was the Messiah.[14]

The second difficulty was that, despite the fact that the country was ruled by the Romans who were consciously seeking to "Romanize" the peoples of the Iberian Peninsula, in a number of places, especially the north, Roman civilization was only a veneer.

---

13 Robert Jewett, "Paul, Phoebe, and the Spanish Mission" in Jacob Neusner, ed., *The Social World of Formative Christianity and Judaism* (Philadelphia, PA: Fortress Press, 1988), 143–144.
14 Jewett, "Paul, Phoebe, and the Spanish Mission," 144.

Greek, the language that Paul had primarily used in the eastern Mediterranean, was only spoken in a few pockets along the Mediterranean coast of Spain. If Paul focused his ministry on the relatively few Greek speakers in the country, it might impede the spread of the gospel. Paul would have needed to use Latin alongside a translator who knew the native languages.[15] This probably meant the apostle was fluent enough in this language to preach and teach. As far as we know, there was no translation of the Old Testament into Latin at this point, so Paul would have needed to translate the Scriptures himself or have an assistant do it.[16]

In planning this mission to Spain, Paul was contemplating something quite different from the missionary work he had previously undertaken. He was going into an utterly pagan environment where there would be substantial linguistic problems. Why was he doing this after two strenuous decades of ministry in the eastern Mediterranean where there was still much to be done?[17]

Understanding Paul

First, there was his belief that his work in the east was winding down. Then, there was his firm conviction that came to expression in 1 Corinthians 9:16: "Woe is me if I do not preach the gospel!" God's calling for Paul's life was that he be a preacher of the gospel to the Gentiles, especially in the northern Mediterranean. If he refused to fulfil this calling, he would know God's displeasure.[18]

But even more importantly, he knew men and women, wherever they lived and whatever their ethnicity, were created to glorify God. In Romans 1, Paul discussed some of the characteristics of sinful Gentile existence. Almost the first one he mentioned was that fallen Gentiles failed to glorify God (Romans 1:21). Now, through the death and resurrection of Jesus, the Lord of glory,

---

15 Jewett, "Paul, Phoebe, and the Spanish Mission," 145–146.
16 Jewett, "Paul, Phoebe, and the Spanish Mission," 146–147.
17 Romans 15:23 should not be understood to mean that there was nowhere else in the northeastern Mediterranean where Paul could preach and that he had evangelized every last town and village in the area. Rather, Paul is indicating that he had fulfilled the mandate of his ministry in this area, which was to establish stable churches in key centres that could then evangelize surrounding towns and villages.
18 See the discussion of this verse by Gordon D. Fee, *The First Epistle to the Corinthians* (Grand Rapids, MI: William B. Eerdmans Publ. Co., 1987), 418–419.

Gentiles *could* glorify God, as Paul had written in an earlier portion of Romans 15:

> Jesus Christ was a servant to the circumcision for the truth of God, to confirm the promises made to the fathers, and that the Gentiles might *glorify* God for his mercy; as it is written, "For this reason I will confess to you among the Gentiles, and sing to your name." And again he says, "Rejoice, O Gentiles, with his people." And again, "Praise the Lord, all you Gentiles! Laud him, all you peoples!" And again, Isaiah says, "There shall be a root of Jesse, and he who shall rise to reign over the Gentiles, in him the Gentiles shall hope" (Romans 15:8–12, italics added).

A divine compulsion to preach the gospel was leading Paul to Spain, so that Gentile men and women might find the reason for their existence. They could live "to glorify God" and—in the words of the *Westminster Shorter Catechism*—"enjoy him forever."

STUDY GUIDE | *Application & reflection*

1. This chapter lists three men in church history who displayed a deep passion for the lost: C.H. Sturgeon, Andrew Fuller and John Bunyan. Who, in history or in your own experience, are those who you look up to as passionate for the salvation of the lost?

2. In Paul's letter to the Romans, he speaks of his desire to come to see them in person. What are Paul's four reasons for this?

3. Paul describes his ministry in Romans 15:20 as one of laying foundations. What does this mean?

4. Paul's vision was to see local churches established as men and women were converted. Why was this important? Why is this important today?

5. What are two main problems Paul would have had to face in evangelizing in Spain?

6. What was Paul's "single-minded commitment"? In what ways is this part of God's call to every believer?

4

Prayer

One of the most fragrant names in the Reformed tradition is that of the nineteenth-century Scottish Free Church minister, Andrew Alexander Bonar (1810–1892). A tireless evangelist and champion of heart religion, he is especially remembered today for his biography of his close friend Robert Murray M'Cheyne (1813–1843) and for the published version of his own diary. Both of these have become spiritual classics. His diary reads like a "treatise on private prayer." For example, on the day of his induction into the pastoral charge of Finnieston Free Church, Glasgow, when he was forty-six, he noted that the Lord had made him feel afresh that "I must be as much with Him alone as with souls in public." A few months after this entry, he wrote these words regarding the importance of prayer: "for nearly ten days past have been much hindered in prayer, and feel my strength weakened thereby. I must at once return, through the Lord's strength, to not less than *three* hours a day spent in prayer and meditation upon the Word."[1] While we are certainly not bound by the details of another's practice, this diary entry emphasizes the vital importance of time for prayer. Bonar placed a high priority on this aspect of the Christian life, a priority he had undoubtedly learned from studying the Word of God.

---

[1] Cited David M. MacIntyre, *The Hidden Life of Prayer* (Tain, Ross-shire: Christian Focus Publications, 1989), xiii.

When the apostles delineate in Acts 6:4 what needed to be priorities in their lives, they mentioned two things in particular: prayer and the ministry of the Word. It is significant that prayer was mentioned first. Likewise, when the apostle Paul concluded his remarks about his future plans in Romans 15, and he asked his readers in Rome to pray for him. He introduced his request with an especially weighty statement:

> Now I beg you, brethren, through the Lord Jesus Christ, and through the love of the Spirit, that you strive together with me in prayers to God for me, that I may be delivered from those in Judaea who do not believe, and that my service for Jerusalem may be acceptable to the saints, that I may come to you with joy by the will of God, and may be refreshed together with you (Romans 15:30–32 NKJV).

The importance that the apostle placed on prayer is found in the solemn way he introduced this passage. He used the word *parakalō*, translated here by the NKJV as "beg," but which can also be rendered "beseech" or "appeal." The same word is found in Romans 12:1, where it is central to that impressive introduction to the entire section on Christian living (Romans 12-15:13), "I beseech you therefore, brethren, by the mercies of God, that you present your bodies...." Paul's repetition of this term in Romans 15:30 indicates something of the priority he wanted his readers to place on prayer.[2] Just as he had appealed to these same readers to present themselves and the entirety of their lives as living sacrifices of worship, so now he urges them to engage meaningfully and regularly in prayer for his ministry.[3] Without such prayer, he intimates, he will be utterly frustrated in his desire to serve God—and ultimately fruitless in his service.

Right from the very beginning of his ministry, Paul knew the importance of personal prayer and of others praying for him.[4] As we look closely at the various elements of this call to prayer in

---

2 Gordon P. Wiles, *Paul's Intercessory Prayers: The Significance of the Intercessory Prayer Passages in the Letters of St Paul* (Cambridge: Cambridge University Press, 1974), 266.
3 Wiles, *Paul's Intercessory Prayers*, 81.
4 See, for example, 1 Thessalonians 5:25 or Colossians 4:2–4.

Romans 15, we must note three things. First of all, the basis upon which Paul appeals for his readers to prayer for him is "the Lord Jesus Christ" and "the love of the Spirit." Second, there is the nature of prayer—it is an arduous, strenuous struggle. Third, there were specific needs for which Paul requested prayer, needs that centred on his ministry in Jerusalem and his eventual trip to Rome.

A two-fold basis for prayer

We noted in Chapter 2 that the basis for Paul's appeal for prayer is, first of all, "through our Lord Jesus Christ." Paul appears to assume two things here. First, if a person is a professing Christian, Paul reckons that he or she is a person who prays. For Paul, to claim that Christ is one's Lord necessarily involves a commitment to prayer. As the seventeenth-century Puritan Richard Baxter (1615–1691) put it: "Prayer is the breath of the new creature."[5] Another Puritan, William Gurnall (1616–1679), declared, "Praying is the same to the new creature as crying is to the natural."[6] A prayerless Christian—a professing Christian who never prays—is a contradiction in terms.

As the Baptist pastor-theologian Andrew Fuller described his early religious experience and his conversion, he noted that in the couple of years prior to his actual conversion, he had a number of deeply emotional, religious experiences. These experiences were accompanied by copious tears, but in the long run, they resulted in no substantial change of lifestyle. Fuller noted that after one of these emotional religious experiences he "lived entirely without prayer and was wedded to my sins just the same as before." After another, he admitted that "he continued in the neglect of prayer" and rightfully concluded that whatever profession he may have made at that time, it could not have been genuine, for to be a Christian is to pray.[7]

Secondly, Paul assumes that Christian prayer is chiefly concerned with the glorification of the triune God and the advance of

---

5 Cited MacIntyre, *The Hidden Life of Prayer*, 20.
6 I.D.E. Thomas, compiled, *A Puritan Golden Treasury* (1975 ed.; repr. Edinburgh: The Banner of Truth Trust, 1977), 209.
7 "Memoir [of Mr. Fuller]" in *The Complete Works of the Rev. Andrew Fuller*, ed. Joseph Belcher, 3rd London ed. (Philadelphia, PA: American Baptist Publication Society, 1845), 1:3–4.

his kingdom. The Lord Jesus, for instance, gives to his disciples some broad guidelines as to what the content of their prayer should be. He mentions, first of all, the exaltation of God and then immediately afterward the advance of his rule in the world: "Our Father in heaven, hallowed be your name. Your Kingdom come. Your will be done on earth as it is in heaven" (Matthew 6:9–10). To be under the authority of Christ compels Christians to pray specifically for the advance of the gospel and the triumph of Christ.

As was also noted in Chapter 2, Paul urged Roman Christians to pray for him "through the love of the Spirit." It was pointed out that this was a unique phrase in the Scriptures. Paul was appealing to the fact that his readers were indwelt by the Spirit of Christ and as such they had experienced the love that the Spirit had given them for other believers. Paul rightly assumed that love for one's brothers and sisters in Christ would naturally mean praying for them.

"Prayer is the gymnasium of the soul"[8]

But prayer is one of the most difficult aspects of the Christian life. We get a glimpse of Paul's recognition of this fact when he goes on to ask the Roman Christians to "strive together with me in prayers to God for me." True intercessory prayer, Paul declares here, involves strain and arduous struggle, the commitment of energy and earnestness. The word underlying the phrase "strive together with me" only occurs here in the New Testament.[9]

Who is this struggle with? First, it is a struggle with the enemy of our souls, Satan, and his demonic hordes. Paul puts it this way in Ephesians 6:12: "We do not wrestle against flesh and blood, but against principalities, against powers, against the rulers of the darkness of this age, against spiritual hosts of wickedness." Satan hates God's people at prayer, for he knows that faithful, persevering prayer is a powerful weapon in the hands of almighty God. As William Cowper (1731–1800), the eighteenth-century poet and hymnwriter, rightly said:

---

[8] A statement of Samuel Zwemer (1867–1952), cited D.A. Carson, *A Call to Spiritual Reformation: Priorities from Paul and His Prayers* (Grand Rapids, MI: Baker Books; Nottingham, UK: Inter-Varsity Press, 1992), 210

[9] A similar idea is found, though, in Colossians 4:12.

Satan trembles when he sees
The weakest saint upon his knees.[10]

But there is also the struggle against the old nature. Listen to
the Puritan preacher John Bunyan describe his own struggle in
prayer:

> May I but speak my own experience, and from that tell you
> the difficulty of praying to God as I ought; it is enough to
> make your poor, blind, carnal men, to entertain strange
> thoughts of me. For, as for my heart, when I go to pray, I find
> it so loth to go to God, and when it is with him, so loth to stay
> with him, that many times I am forced in my prayers; *first* to
> beg God that he would take mine heart, and set it on himself
> in Christ, and when it is there, that he would keep it there
> (Psalm 86.11). Nay, many times I know not what to pray for,
> I am so blind, nor how to pray, I am so ignorant; only (blessed
> be grace) the *Spirit helps our infirmities.*
>
> Oh, the starting-holes that the heart hath in time of prayer!
> None knows how many by-ways the heart hath, and back-
> lanes, to slip away from the presence of God.[11]

This passage displays some of the most attractive features of
Puritan writers like Bunyan: their transparency and their in-depth
knowledge of the human heart. From personal experience, Bunyan
well knew the allergic reaction of the sinful nature to the presence
of God that still resided in the bosom of every believer. Instead of
coming into God's radiant presence to pray, believers sometimes
want to run and hide, like Adam after he had sinned in the garden.
In other words, prayer demands discipline and hard work.

Prayer is a struggle. But Paul expected believers to persevere in
prayer and know something of the victory of persevering, faithful
prayer. Why did he expect this? Because Christians are indwelt by
the Spirit of Christ. He had already used this fact as part of his
appeal to the Roman Christians to engage in prayer on his behalf.

---

10 William Cowper, "Exhortation to Prayer" in his and John Newton, *Olney Hymns, in
Three Books,* 7th ed. (London: J. Johnson, 1802), 199 (Book II, Hymn LX).

11 John Bunyan, *I Will Pray with the Spirit, and I Will Pray with the Understanding also: or,
A Discourse Touching Prayer,* 2nd ed. (London, 1663), 51–52.

If he were pressed to give a reason for why he expects Christians to know a good measure of victory and consistency in prayer, the Spirit and the Spirit's power would surely figure largely in his answer. Were it not for the Spirit, none would be able to persevere in prayer. "A man without the help of the Spirit," Bunyan once declared, "cannot so much as pray once; much less, continue…in a sweet praying frame."[12]

Certain specific requests for prayer

Paul had three things that he wanted the Romans to pray for on his behalf:

1. To be kept safe from those fanatical Jews in Judea who hated the gospel and who would dearly love to see Paul dead.

2. For the collection of money which he had gathered from the Gentile churches for the "saints in Jerusalem" (Romans 15:26–27) to be well received by the Jerusalem church and thus his goal of displaying the unity of Jew and Gentile in Christ achieved.

3. For him to eventually come to Rome and find rest and refreshment among them. Note: he was not asking for a holiday in Rome—but spiritual refreshment found in the context of fellowship and preparation for further ministry (see Romans 15:24, 28). This was the reason for the first two requests: what drove the first two requests was his hunger to further extend the reach of the gospel.

This final request in verse 32 indicates he expected his time in Jerusalem to be fraught with tension and danger. While thoroughly convinced it was God's will for him to go to Jerusalem and fully acquainted with the dangers of going there, he was by no means reckless and eager to throw his life away. Thus, he asked his brothers and sisters to seek his protection through prayer.

---

12 Bunyan, *I Will Pray with the Spirit*, 56.

D.A. Carson, in some applicatory comments on this text, rightly notes that we need to pray for Christian leaders to be preserved
in the face of opponents seeking to destroy their ministries. Carson
also argues, on the basis of this passage in Romans 15, that "we
should pray that Christian leaders might find that their Christian
service is acceptable to those to whom they minister."[13]

2 Thessalonians 3:1-2

It is fascinating to note that five or so years earlier, Paul had made
a similar request for prayer to believers in Thessalonica. Writing
from the city of Corinth, he had asked the Thessalonian Christians
to "pray for us, that the word of the Lord may run swiftly and be
glorified, just as it is with you, and that we may be delivered
from unreasonable and wicked men; for all have not faith"
(2 Thessalonians 3:1-2). As these Thessalonian believers had
prayed, God moved in the city of Corinth. Their prayers brought
revival and protection for Paul from Jewish leaders who wanted
him expelled from the city. Their prayers even caused a Roman
governor, Gallio, to unwittingly befriend the church in that city
(see Acts 18:12-16).[14]

On Paul's trip to Jerusalem, things turned out quite differently.
Paul was nearly killed in a riot in the Temple. He ended up a prisoner of the Roman state. He languished in prison in Palestine for
close to two years. There was then a perilous voyage to Rome and
a further two-year period of imprisonment in the Roman capital
(Acts 21-28). Would Paul have concluded God did not answer his
people's prayers? No, not at all. Notice in Romans 15:32 those
tremendously important words: "by the will of God." Prayer, as
the apostle thinks of it, and as the Scriptures attest, is never a pre-
sumptuous demanding of God. It is always done with the recognition that God answers his people's prayers in his own ways and in
his own time.

Mature prayers never leave God's sovereignty out of the picture.
This deep sense of God's sovereign control over the events of his

---

[13] D.A. Carson, *A Call to Spiritual Reformation: Priorities from Paul and His Prayers*
(Grand Rapids, MI: Baker Books, 1992), 216-219.
[14] For a discussion of this event, see Michael A.G. Haykin, "Praying for Revival: Is It
Biblical?," *Reformation Today* 115 (May-June 1990): 10-14. For an overview of Paul's
requests for prayer for himself, see the addendum to this chapter.

life does not issue in an attitude of fatalism, where prayer is regarded as next to useless. On the contrary, Paul knew that God's sovereign purposes were regularly accomplished through the prayers of his people. Thomas Blundell (c.1752–1824), an eighteenth-century British Baptist and friend of William Carey, well expressed Paul's conviction when he stated,

> It is chiefly in answer to prayer that God has carried on his cause in the world: he could work without any such means; but he does not, neither will he.... He loves that his people should feel interested in his cause, and labour to promote it, though he himself worketh all in all.[15]

Prayer and mission are vitally and inextricably intertwined.[16]

---

15 Thomas Blundell, *The River of Life Impeded in his Sermons on Various Subjects* (London: J. Burditt, 1806), 183–184.

16 See the popular exploration of this key principle by Helen Jean Parks, *Holding the Ropes* (Nashville, TN: Broadman Press, 1983). Parks' title comes, or is drawn, from the famous statement by Andrew Fuller that William Carey's intention to go to India as a missionary was akin to descending into a gold mine, let down by a rope. If Carey were to go, Fuller promised, he and his friends would "hold the rope." Such rope-holding definitely included prayer. For the story, see Mary E. Farwell, *The Life of William Carey* (Chicago, IL: Women's Presbyterian Board of Mission of the Northwest, 1888), 20; S. Pearce Carey, *William Carey*, ed. Peter Masters (London: The Wakeman Trust, 1993), 108.

ADDENDUM 1
Paul's prayer requests for himself

Romans 15:30 is not the only place where the apostle Paul asks prayer for himself. Here are the others:[17]

1. Prayer for God's help when he and members of his apostolic circle proclaimed the good news about Jesus Christ:
   • that God would provide the opportunity for him (and those with him) to speak and be heard (Colossians 4:3).
   • that he would know what to say (Ephesians 6:19).
   • that he would proclaim the message clearly (Colossians 4:4).
   • that he would be bold, not afraid, as he proclaimed the message (Ephesians 6:19–20).
   • that the message of the gospel would spread and be honoured (2 Thessalonians 3:1).

2. Prayer that the Gentile Christians' collection of money for the poor Jewish believers in Jerusalem would be accepted by them (Romans 15:31).

3. Prayer for deliverance from people who opposed him:
   • for deliverance from those who did not trust God (2 Thessalonians 3:2).
   • for deliverance from unbelieving Jews in Judea (Romans 15:30).

4. Prayer for deliverance from difficult circumstances and imprisonment:
   • for deliverance from severe hardships (2 Corinthians 1:11). Paul expressed the hope that due to their

---

[17] This Addendum is taken from Dennis Hinks, "Paul's Prayers–An Example for Us To Follow–What Do You Pray About?–Part 3–Paul's Prayer Requests for Himself" (https://www.journal33.org/lovegod/html/p-pray3.html; accessed April 9, 2022). Used with the kind permission of Dennis Hinks.

prayers, God would deliver him (and his friends) and, when this happened, many others would then be able to express gratitude to God for that deliverance.

- for deliverance from chains and death (Philippians 1:19). Paul expected that, because of their prayers, the Spirit of Jesus Christ would use the things that had happened for his deliverance. However, his primary desire was to exalt Christ under any circumstances, whether that meant life or death (Philippians 1:20).
- for his release from prison (Philemon 1:22). He expected God to grant what they prayed, so he told them to get ready for his return.

5. Prayer that he would be able to visit the people to whom he was writing:
   - so he could be a blessing to them so that they might become spiritually stronger. He hoped that they could be encouraged by each other's faith (Romans 1:10–12; see also Romans 15:32).
   - so he could help them grow even further in their faith (1 Thessalonians 3:10).

In summary:
We should make it our desire to pray for others who are being used by God. When we do so, we are in a sense, right there with them. As Paul told the Roman Christians, when they prayed for him, they were joining him in his "struggle" (Romans 15:30) in his work for the kingdom of God.[18]

---

[18] Hinks, "Paul's Prayers."

STUDY GUIDE | *Application & reflection*

1. Paul placed a high priority on prayer. In Romans 15, what are some of the reasons Paul wanted the believers in Rome to pray for him?

2. This chapter notes Paul's twofold basis for prayer. What are these? How do these two things impact your prayer life? In what ways are you learning from Paul about prayer?

3. Paul acknowledged prayer can be a difficult, arduous struggle. What are some things that make it hard for you to pray?

4. Persevering in prayer can be hard. How can we be helped in this?

5. What are some ways you can pray specifically for Christian leaders in your life?

6. According to this chapter, "Mature prayers never leave God's sovereignty out of the picture." Elaborate on this statement.

5

Co-workers

I n the list of greetings to brothers and sisters whom Paul knew in the house churches of Rome, he said this about two of them: "Greet Priscilla and Aquila my fellow workers in Christ Jesus, who risked their own necks for my life, to whom not only I give thanks, but also all the churches of the Gentiles" (Romans 16:3–4). What an amazing statement! This brother and sister, Aquila and Priscilla, so loved the apostle Paul that they were willing to die for him. In fact, as you read the apostle Paul's letters attentively, you find a small group of men who willingly gave up their plans and their ambitions to see Paul's apostolic calling fulfilled. Paul's ministry took place within the context of a circle of like-minded brothers and sisters. A common stereotype of Paul is that he was a sort of "lone ranger" evangelist, one who preferred to work by himself. In fact, Paul was a man rarely found without companions. Paul was a very gregarious man, one who clearly delighted in the company of his fellow believers.[1] This can be readily seen in a number of texts. Let's look first at Colossians 4:7–18 and then Colossians 1:1.

Tychicus

One of the most significant members of the Pauline circle was Tychicus. Chronologically, we first meet him in Acts 20:4, where Luke tells us that Tychicus was from the Roman province of Asia,

---

[1] F.F. Bruce, *Paul: Apostle of the Heart Set Free* (Grand Rapids, MI: William B. Eerdmans Publ. Co., 1977), 457.

probably from the city of Ephesus. Then, we find the references to him in Colossians 4:7–9.[2] First, notice the way Paul describes him as "a beloved brother." The bond between Paul and his co-workers was the love of Christ, which made them "beloved brothers." Tychicus is also described as "a faithful servant and fellow slave in the Lord." Paul trusted him to take the letter to Colossae and faithfully communicate to the Colossians all they needed to know about Paul (Colossians 4:8). It is important to note that he knew how to encourage the brothers. Not all servants of God have such a gift or temperament. Some are gloom and doom. Not so Tychicus.

Since Tychicus was such a trusted brother, Paul could count on him to faithfully deliver the letter to the Colossian church. Tychicus may also have been the person to read it aloud at the worship service in the house churches at Colossae and Laodicea (see Colossians 4:16). If so, this would speak of his ability as a reader. It is not easy to determine how many people in the ancient world could read.[3] The ability to read was largely limited to about ten to twelve per cent of the total population, primarily the senatorial, equestrian and upper middle classes. Part of this was because "Greco-Roman religions were not centered around a sacred text; there was no holy writ to be studied, copied, memorized, and transmitted."[4] Since there was a long tradition of the importance of literacy, among first-century Jewish communities the percentage of people able to read would have been somewhat higher. This brings to mind, for example, passages like Psalm 119 that sought to develop a spirituality of the Word among God's people in general.

Clearly, even if Tychicus himself did not read the letter to the Colossians, he would make sure this was carried out, since he was a "faithful minister." Paul's instructions in Colossians 4:16 were significant; he directed them to read this letter aloud during the corporate gathering of the church. This speaks to the letter's authority. Paul also urged Tychicus to read the letter to the church

---

2 See also the nearly identical remarks in Ephesians 6:21–22.

3 E. Randolph Richards, "Will the Real Author Please Stand Up? The Author in Greco-Roman Letter Writing" in *Come Let Us Reason: New Essays in Christian Apologetics*, ed. Paul Copan and William Lane Craig (Nashville, TN: B&H, 2012), 123.

4 Moyer V. Hubbard, *Christianity in the Greco-Roman World* (Grand Rapids, MI: Baker, 2010), 69.

at Laodicea, which was 10 miles from Colossae, and that they also read the letter from Laodicea.

Later, after Paul's release from Roman imprisonment (described in Acts 28), Tychicus stayed with Paul, even to the very close of the apostle's ministry.[5] In fact, Tychicus was probably the bearer of the letter we call 2 Timothy to Timothy at Ephesus.

Three Jewish Christians

Colossians 4 also mentions three Jewish believers. First, Aristarchus, whom Paul calls "my fellow prisoner."[6] He is mentioned initially in Acts 19:29, having been seized during a riot in Ephesus. In Acts 20:4, we learn he was a Thessalonian believer. He stuck with Paul through the time of his arrest in Jerusalem and his initial imprisonment in Caesarea. Then he sailed with Paul to Rome (Acts 27:1–2). In fact, this is a strong indication that the letter to the Colossians was written from Rome. Aristarchus obviously then stayed in Rome during Paul's imprisonment there.[7]

We then have the mention of Mark, the cousin of Barnabas. There is a great story here. We find the first mention of Mark in Acts 12:12, when a prayer meeting for the release of the apostle Peter from prison was held at his mother house. Mark is explicitly connected to Paul in Acts 12:25, where we find he accompanied Paul with his cousin Barnabas on a ministry trip to Antioch. In Acts 13, when Paul and Barnabas undertook what is called Paul's first missionary trip, Mark accompanied them. For some unspecified reason, he abandoned them halfway through (Acts 13:13). This abandonment caused a rift between Paul and Barnabas, as we discover in Acts 15:36–40. Paul was now preparing to embark on his second major missionary trip. Although Barnabas wanted to take Mark with them, Paul was insistent he not accompany them as he had abandoned them in the middle of the previous missionary trip (Acts 15:38). The disagreement between Paul and Barnabas was so sharp the two Christian leaders parted company.[8] As Colossians 4:10 indicates, Barnabas presumably was able to help Mark redeem

---

[5] See, in this regard, Titus 3:12 and 2 Timothy 4:12.

[6] Colossians 4:10.

[7] Peter T. O'Brien, *Colossians, Philemon*, Word Biblical Commentary, vol. 44 (Waco, TX: Word Books, 1982), 249–250.

[8] Luke uses the word *paroxysmos* to describe their falling out in Acts 15:39.

his reputation, for Mark was now part of the Pauline circle once again. Indeed, in Philemon 24, written around the same time as Colossians, Paul calls Mark his "fellow worker." Paul's high regard for him continued till the end of the apostle's life, as he testifies in 2 Timothy 4:11, Mark "is useful to me in the ministry" (CSB).[9]

The third Jewish Christian mentioned in this passage is Jesus Justus (Colossians 4:11). We know nothing about this brother apart from this reference. Note the way Paul describes the ministry of Jesus Justus, along with that of Aristarchus and Mark. He is a fellow worker for the kingdom of God. The term "the kingdom of God," or "the reign of God," is one Paul employs some dozen times and for him it has both present and future aspects. It can be used to depict the believer's present experience of life in the Spirit (Romans 14:17), but it is also something future (1 Corinthians 6:9). Like Aristarchus and Mark, Jesus Justus had also been a great comfort to Paul. The word "comfort" only occurs here in the New Testament; it is often found outside of the New Testament in epitaphs. In other words, Jesus Justus had helped Paul find comfort in the face of possible death.[10]

Three Gentile believers

Paul mentions three Gentile believers. First, there is Luke, whom Paul identifies as "the beloved physician" (Colossians 4:14). Luke is the man who has been traditionally identified as the author of the Gospel of Luke and the Book of Acts. He joined the Pauline band of co-workers in the middle of the second missionary journey (see Acts 16:10).[11] Then there is Demas, who is remembered usually for his abandonment of Paul during his final imprisonment (2 Timothy 4:10).[12] The main figure among these three Gentile believers, though, is Epaphras.

Usually, Paul wrote letters to churches he himself had planted; not so with the letter to the Romans nor with the letter to the

---

9 Mark is also found as a helper of Peter in 1 Peter 5:13. The Gospel of Mark is traditionally attributed to him.

10 O'Brien, *Colossians, Philemon*, 251–252.

11 Paul also mentions him by name in 2 Timothy 4:11.

12 The exact meaning of the description of this abandonment in 2 Timothy 4:10—"he loved this present world"—has been debated down through the centuries. Did he simply bail on Paul, or is Paul implying he has apostatized?

Colossians. Paul did not found the church at Colossae (see Colossians 2:1). Paul, in fact, had only heard about their faith (Colossians 1:4, 9). He had not been with them in person. The individual who told Paul about the Colossian church was the man who appears to have been the key church planter in the region of Colossae, namely, Epaphras (Colossians 1:5–8).[13]

Epaphras is mentioned three times by name in the New Testament: Colossians 1:7; 4:12; and Philemon 23. Note the significant ways Paul describes him. First, there is Colossians 1:7 where Paul calls him a "beloved fellow slave (*syndoulou*)." The use of the term "beloved" here speaks of Paul's love for him. Like Paul, he is a slave (*doulos*) of Jesus Christ.[14] In Colossians 1:7, Paul also calls Epaphras "a faithful/trustworthy minister," which clearly indicates the teaching Epaphras gave to the Colossians (see 1:5–8) was faithful to the apostolic gospel. The geographical scope of his ministry is described in Colossians 4:13: Colossae, Laodicea and Hierapolis. If we wish to describe his ministry, Ephesians 4:11 captures it well: he is an evangelist, for at least three house churches were formed through his ministry:

- a house church in Colossae (Philemon 1–2).
- a church in Laodicea (Colossians 4:15). Nympha was probably a woman, though it could be used as a short form for Nymphodorus.[15] In fact, there may have been two house churches in Laodicea: that of the brothers and that of Nympha.[16]

---

13 Larry J. Kreitzer has penned a helpful study of Epaphras—though I disagree with some of his arguments: see "Epaphras and Philip: The Undercover Evangelists of Hierapolis" in *"You Will Be My Witnesses": A Festschrift in Honor of the Reverend D. Allison A. Trites on the Occasion of His Retirement*, ed. R. Glenn Wooden, Timothy R. Ashley and Robert S. Wilson (Macon, GA: Mercer University Press, 2003), 127–143.

14 To translate *syndoulou* as "fellow servant" misses the impact of the word "slave (*doulos*)." Note also Philemon 23, which describes Epaphras as a "fellow prisoner." The term here "fellow prisoner" actually means "prisoner of war." As a prisoner of the Roman state, Epaphras would not be able to return to the congregations in the Lycus Valley, hence, Paul will be sending another of the Pauline circle, Tychicus, to Colossae with the letter (see Colossians 4:7–8).

15 O'Brien, *Colossians, Philemon*, 258.

16 Murray J. Harris, *Exegetical Guide to the Greek New Testament: Colossians and Philemon* (Nashville, TN: B&H Academic, 2010), 181–182.

- a church in Hierapolis, which is not mentioned specifically by Paul.

According to Colossians 4:12, Epaphras is "one of you," which tells us that Epaphras is a Colossian. Like most of the Christians at Colossae, he probably came from a pagan background. There were a considerable number of Jews in the Lycus Valley, but it was mainly former pagans who formed the bulk of the church.[17] There are indications in the letter regarding the pagan roots of most of the believers in Colossae. For example, look at the list of vices in Colossians 3:5—these vices are distinctively pagan ones. Look at the description Paul uses for the state of the Colossian believers before conversion: they "were dead...in the uncircumcision of [their] flesh" (Colossians 2:13). The word "uncircumcision" is more likely to be used of Gentiles rather than Jews.[18] Epaphras shares in this background. A final note about Epaphras: It could be the case that he was converted through Paul's ministry.[19]

Paul's view of the ministry of Epaphras is clarified by his comparision of his own ministry (Colossians 1:29) to that of Epaphras (Colossians 4:12). Paul uses the identical verb, "striving" or "wrestling" (*agōnizomenos*), in both cases. Both have experienced Christian ministry as a place of strenuous effort, indeed, wrestling for the souls of men and women. Epaphras undergirded his ministry of evangelism and church planting with prayer, wrestling on behalf of the Colossians, something we saw in the previous chapter as a mark of Paul's own prayer life.[20]

Timothy

One last co-worker who needs mentioning is named in Colossians 1:1, where Paul includes Timothy as the co-author of the letter to the Colossian church. In other words, Paul penned this letter with Timothy. Timothy may have acted as Paul's scribe, for he

---

[17] O'Brien, *Colossians, Philemon*, xxvii.
[18] C.F.D. Moule, *The Epistles of Paul the Apostle to the Colossians and to Philemon*, The Cambridge Greek Testament Commentary (Cambridge: Cambridge University Press, 1957), 29; O'Brien, *Colossians, Philemon*, xxviii–xxix.
[19] Moule, *Paul the Apostle to the Colossians and to Philemon*, 27.
[20] As C.F.D. Moule puts it, "On the nature and scope of Christian prayer there is much to be learnt from Colossians" (*Paul the Apostle to the Colossians and to Philemon*, 10).

usually used an *amanuensis*, a literary assistant, in writing his letters.[21] Although he was probably twenty or so years Paul's junior, Timothy had become the apostle's closest friend and a key figure in the Pauline circle. In the words of F.F. Bruce, Timothy

> readily surrendered whatever personal ambitions he might have cherished in order to play the part of a son to Paul and help him in his missionary activity, showing a selfless concern for others that matched the apostle's own eagerness to spend and be spent for them.[22]

We first meet Timothy in AD 48/49 (Acts 15:36–16:5). One of Luke's favourite devices in Acts is to emphasize by means of contrast. Consider for example Acts 4:32–5:11, where Barnabas' true generosity is contrasted with the pretense of Ananias and Sapphira. In Acts 18:24–19:7, Apollos' experience of the Spirit is contrasted with that of the Ephesian disciples. So here, at the close of Acts 15 and the beginning of Acts 16, Paul does not wish to take John Mark as a potential mentee; instead, he finds Timothy. What is important to note is Paul's intentionality with regard to future leadership. He did not simply sit back and assume that since true Christian leadership was a gift of the Spirit he did not need to do anything. Rather, just as he had taken John Mark with himself and Barnabas on his first missionary journey, so here, he approached the elders in the church at either Derbe or Lystra regarding the suitability of Timothy.

Timothy was young at the time, probably in his early twenties.[23] Timothy came from a mixed marriage. His mother, Eunice (2 Timothy 1:5), a believer, had with her mother, Lois (2 Timothy 1:5), taught Timothy the Scriptures (2 Timothy 3:15). His father was a Greek and, based on Luke's description of his home life in Acts 16:1, not a believer. This conclusion is supported in 2 Timothy, which does not mention his father at all. Since Timothy

---

[21] See Romans 16:22, where Paul's scribe, Tertius, actually names himself. See also the Addendum to this chapter, that has a small discussion of Tertius.

[22] Bruce, *Paul*, 457.

[23] See 1 Timothy 4:12, which was written around AD 63/64, where Paul makes reference to Timothy's youth. In Greek thought, a man was young till he was forty.

had a good reputation in his home church, he was commissioned to go with Paul.[24]

Despite the difference in their ages, the two friends shared the same goals to the full. One sees this especially in Philippians 2:19–22. The Philippian church evidently had been experiencing some measure of disunity. Paul mentions it explicitly in the final chapter of the letter, when he urges Euodia and Syntyche "to be of the same mind in the Lord (*to auto phronein en kyriō*)" (Philippians 4:2). In chapter 2, Paul devotes a lengthy section of this letter to resolving this problem. He begins in Philippians 2:2 by urging the Philippians to be "likeminded (*to auto phronēte*)"—the same phrase Paul employs in Philippians 4:2—"have the same love, be in full accord and of one mind (*to hen phronountes*)…looking out for not only their own interests but also those of others" (Philippians 2:2, 4).

To illustrate this powerful set of gospel admonitions and drive them home, Paul encouraged the Philippians to meditate on the example of Christ, whose mind and heart was focused not on his own personal interests but on those of fallen humanity. So taken up was Christ with the plight of sinners that though he was fully God he "made himself of no reputation." He became incarnate and willingly and humbly took upon himself the burden of human sin and was "obedient to the point of death, even the death of the cross" (Philippians 2:6–8).

After outlining the work and motivation of Christ as an example to imitate, the apostle Paul returns to this theme of thinking of others' best interests in Philippians 2:19–22. Here he gives another example of being likeminded and having the interests of others at heart. This time, he turns to his friend Timothy.

> I hope in the Lord Jesus to send Timothy to you soon, so that I too may be cheered by news of you. For I have no one like him, who will be genuinely concerned for your welfare. They all seek their own interests, not those of Jesus Christ. But you

---

[24] 1 Timothy 4:14, which tell us that at his commissioning or ordination, it was revealed that Timothy was indeed gifted for ministry—we are not told what the gift was exactly. This event may be in view in 1 Timothy 6:12. For Timothy's gifts, see the next chapter.

know Timothy's proven worth, how as a son with a father he has served with me in the gospel.

From the words and phrases Paul uses here it is clear he is recommending Timothy as an example of Christlikeness. Paul knew that Timothy, unlike others, sincerely cared for the state of the Philippians. He was genuinely concerned about the needs of other believers and was not solely seeking to promote his own interests. It should be noted, Paul used the identical language of Timothy that he used of Christ.[25] As such, he displays the mind of Christ. Paul can thus describe Timothy in verse 20 as "likeminded"— because of his desire to be like Christ. Timothy was one who fully shares Paul's heart and mind and is thus a completely trustworthy companion and friend of Paul.

Because of their age difference, Paul naturally speaks of Timothy as his son. He says Timothy has proven his worth during his ministry with Paul "as a son with his father" (Philippians 2:22). But he quickly adds, Timothy has not been serving *him* but the *gospel.* Paul was always very careful to avoid giving the impression that he was lord and master over the faith of others.[26] Timothy did not serve him, but together—as equals before God—they served the Lord of the gospel, Christ.

At the heart of the Pauline mission was a circle of friends bound together by their love for Christ, his people and the extension of his reign.

---

[25] Compare Philippians 2:4 and 21
[26] In this regard, see how he approaches Philemon in his epistle to the Colossian believers. I consider Paul's letter to Philemon enormously helpful in understanding Paul as a leader.

ADDENDUM 2
On Tertius

Among the Pauline circle is a man whose name appears but once in the apostle's letters. It is Tertius and his name is found in Romans 16:22, where we read, "I Tertius, who wrote this letter [that is, the letter to the Romans] greet you [that is the believers in the church at Rome] in the Lord."[27] It is obvious that Tertius is not the author of this letter, which has had a massive impact on the history of the church down through the centuries. The author is indisputably Paul, as Romans 1:1 clearly indicates. Who then is Tertius, and what does he mean when he says, "I...wrote this letter"?

First of all, Tertius is what is technically known as an *amanuensis*, one to whom Paul would have dictated the letter to the Christians at Rome. Tertius would have written down the inspired words of the apostle. Our society takes literacy, the ability to write and read, for granted. How many people, though, could write in the world in which the New Testament was written, that is the world of first-century Judaism and the Roman Empire? How many of them could read, a skill not necessarily conjoined to the ability to write? These seemingly simple questions are actually not easy to answer. William V. Harris, in a definitive study of literacy in the ancient world, concludes that while literacy levels in the Roman world would have differed from region to region, overall literacy was around ten to fifteen percent.[28] The level may have been somewhat higher in Jewish communities where the written word played a more central role than in Græco-Roman society. The fact that Tertius could write—which would also have meant that he could

---

27 The Greek could be translated: "I Tertius, who wrote this letter in the Lord, greet you."

28 See the discussion by William V. Harris, *Ancient Literacy* (Cambridge, MA; London: Harvard University Press, 1989), 248–284.

read—placed him among a small elite of literate individuals within the Roman Empire.

Furthermore, the fact that Paul asked Tertius to play the role he did in writing down the letter to the Romans indicates Tertius had graceful penmanship. Not every writer's handwriting was easily legible.[29] However, Paul's use of Tertius, and probably other *amanuenses*,[30] indicates he did not deem his own handwriting sufficiently good enough to pen an entire letter. Tertius is thus almost definitely a professionally trained writer who had a fine penmanship and an ear for dictation.[31]

---

[29] Paul himself mentions his handwriting on a number of occasions. Usually near the very end of the letter, he would take up the pen to write a few words. See, for example, Galatians 6:11; 1 Corinthians 16:21; Colossians 4:18; Philemon 19; and 2 Thessalonians 3:17.

[30] As we saw in this chapter, Timothy may well have functioned as Paul's *amanuensis* in the writing of Colossians.

[31] See C.E.B. Cranfield, *A Critical and Exegetical Commentary on the Epistle to the Romans* (Edinburgh: T & T Clark Ltd., 1975), I, 2–5.

STUDY GUIDE | *Application & reflection*

1. Paul was not a "lone ranger" Christian. He had fellow-workers alongside him throughout his ministry. What was special about Tychicus?

2. Paul speaks of three Jewish Christian companions in the faith in Colossians 4. List each one and describe the ways they were a help to Paul.

3. Paul also mentions three Gentile believers who were a help to him. List each one and describe Paul's relationship with them.

4. How might you find such friends in the faith? What hinders this experience in your life?

5. Paul's relationship with Timothy was of a father to a son. They had a strong bond. Describe their relationship and the ways God used it in both their lives.

6. How might you pursue a mentoring relationship with a younger or older believer? Think specifically of your situation: Who comes to mind? What are some steps you can take to build mentoring and gospel friendships into your life?

6

The Spirit[†]

One of the ever-recurring features of human history is war. Often fed by human love of empire, desire for domination, ethnic pride or hatred of other peoples, men go into battle to kill or be killed. Wives are widowed, young women lose their sweethearts, children their fathers, parents their sons, sisters their brothers.[1] Yet as terrible as war is, I do not believe the Bible teaches that Christians must be pacifists. When John the Baptist, for instance, was asked by some soldiers what kind of lives they should live that befit those who were repentant of their sin, John told them: "Do not extort money from anyone by threats or by false accusation, and be content with your wages."[2] Nothing is said about leaving the army. And Paul, when dealing with the realities of political life in Romans 13, declared that the state has the right to exercise capital punishment.[3] Christian theologians from Augustine onward have argued this text implies that the use of violence by the state in self-defense is not illegitimate and there is such a thing as a "just war."[4]

[†] Nearly all of this chapter has appeared in Michael A.G. Haykin, *The Empire of the Holy Spirit: Reflections on Biblical and Historical Patterns of Life in the Spirit*, 3rd ed. (Peterborough, ON: H&E Publishing, 2020) and appears here by kind permission of H&E Publishing.

[1] As I write these words, the Russo-Ukrainian War is raging with all of the attendant horrors of modern warfare.

[2] Luke 3:14.

[3] Romans 13:1–4.

[4] See Augustine's *Letter* 189 for a succinct presentation of his position.

In the Old Testament, war is recognized as part of the reality of living in that unique situation when God was in covenant with a nation, namely the people of Israel. In Deuteronomy 20, God laid down rules on how his ancient covenant people were to conduct themselves in war. Heading the list was the command that, when they went into battle, they were to trust unconditionally in the Lord and his mighty power:

> When you go out to war against your enemies, and see horses and chariots and an army larger than your own, you shall not be afraid of them, for the Lord your God is with you, who brought you up out of the land of Egypt. And when you draw near to the battle, the priest shall come forward and speak to the people and shall say to them, 'Hear, O Israel, today you are drawing near for battle against your enemies: let not your heart faint. Do not fear or panic or be in dread of them, for the Lord your God is he who goes with you to fight for you against your enemies, to give you the victory.'[5]

In the new covenant era, God's people are also engaged in a war. This war is not one involving earthly weapons, battles with earthly armies, the conquest of nations or the killing of human beings. As the Lord Jesus told the Roman governor Pilate, whose rule in Judaea was supported by the military might of the Roman Imperium:

> My kingdom is not of this world. If my kingdom were of this world, my servants would have been fighting, that I might not be delivered over to the Jews. But my kingdom is not from the world.[6]

Paul repeats this theme: "though we walk in the flesh, we are not waging war according to the flesh."[7] Similar to the warfare of the Old Testament, the warfare in which the church is engaged also has its rules. The first is identical to what has been cited in

---

[5] Deuteronomy 20:1–4.
[6] John 18:36.
[7] 2 Corinthians 10:3.

Deuteronomy: trust wholeheartedly in the Lord and his almighty power. One place such wholehearted trust is inculcated is in the first chapter of 2 Timothy.

The historical context of 2 Timothy

2 Timothy, as Gordon Fee states, is "a kind of last will and testament, a passing on of the mantle" from Paul to Timothy.[8] Paul had been arrested again, probably in Asia Minor. Timothy was still in Asia Minor, in the city of Ephesus.[9] Certain Christian leaders in the Roman province of Asia, whom Paul names—Phygelus and Hermogenes—and whom he expected to have helped him, had deserted him[10] and he was in prison in Rome.[11] He had undergone a kind of preliminary trial to determine if there was enough evidence to take him to a full trial.[12] This first trial may have been presided over by Gaius Ofonius Tigellinus (c. AD 10–69), the notorious and vicious head of the Praetorian Guard. Paul referred to coming through that first trial as having been "rescued from the lion's mouth."[13] At that defence, though, Paul expected he would have been supported by some of the believers in Rome, but they had apparently failed him.[14]

Although he survived that first trial, Paul was quite certain of what would be the final outcome of the trial process: his condemnation and death.[15] He thus urged Timothy to come as fast as he could to Rome, which meant sailing from Ephesus before the winter storms made navigating the Mediterranean dangerous, something Paul, a seasoned traveller of the Mediterranean, knew all too well.[16] But in case Timothy would not reach Rome before

---

8 Gordon D. Fee, *1 and 2 Timothy, Titus*, New International Biblical Commentary, rev. ed. (San Francisco, CA: Harper & Row, 1988), xxv.

9 2 Timothy 1:16–18; 4:19.

10 2 Timothy 1:15.

11 2 Timothy 1:16–17; 2:9.

12 2 Timothy 4:16.

13 2 Timothy 4:17.

14 2 Timothy 4:16. Are these the Christians whom Paul names in 2 Timothy 4:21?

15 2 Timothy 4:6–8.

16 2 Timothy 4:9, 21. For one of Paul's voyages on the Mediterranean that involved a shipwreck, see Acts 27–28. In 2 Corinthians 11:25–26 Paul mentions being in danger while on the sea and specifically being shipwrecked three times, on one occasion spending "a night and a day" adrift at sea.

Paul's execution, Paul used the written word in place of the spoken word to urge Timothy to guard the gospel from theological error, to stay true to what he had been taught and to be faithful in preaching the Word.[17]

The latter admonitions were also necessary because Paul was deeply concerned about a problem in the church at Ephesus that was equally as serious as persecution by the Roman state. There were leaders in the house churches of Ephesus who had fallen into grave error. In a departure from his normal method of dealing with theological errorists, Paul named two of these leaders: Hymenaeus and Philetus.[18] The things these men were teaching were not at all promoting the spiritual health of the believers in Ephesus. On the contrary, Paul could only liken their teaching to "gangrene" for it had a dangerous tendency to spread falsehood to believers just as gangrene infects and eats up neighbouring tissue.[19]

What errors were these leaders teaching? Paul mentions only one specifically: the denial of the bodily resurrection.[20] Hymenaeus and Philetus probably shared a common Greek conviction that only the soul was of true value and the body was to be shed at death like a useless shell.[21] If so, their teaching seems to have anticipated the errors of the Gnostics of the second century who despised the body and refused to believe it could be included in redemption.[22]

In John Owen's (1616–1683) final letter before his death on August 24, 1683, he told a close friend, "I am leaving the ship of the church in a storm," a reference to the persecution that

---

17 2 Timothy 1:14; 3:14–15; 4:2.

18 2 Timothy 2:17. See also 1 Timothy 1:18–20.

19 J.N.D. Kelly, *A Commentary on the Pastoral Epistles: Timothy I & II, and Titus* (1960 ed.; repr. Peabody, MA: Hendrickson Publishers, 1987), 184; Philip H. Towner, *The Letters to Timothy and Titus* (Grand Rapids, MI; Cambridge, U.K.: William B. Eerdmans Publ. Co., 2006), 525.

20 2 Timothy 2:17–18. For other probable reflections on these false teachers, see 2 Timothy 2:14 and 16, which mentions quarrelling about words and "irreverent babble," and 2 Timothy 2:23, which refers to "foolish, ignorant controversies." 2 Timothy 3:1–9 may also refer to these men. On the "irreverent babble," see also 1 Timothy 6:20–21.

21 For a different theological reconstruction of the error in view here, see Towner, *Letters to Timothy and Titus*, 526–529.

22 Another element of the errors at Ephesus, the rejection of marriage (1 Timothy 4:1–3), also anticipates second-century Gnosticism.

Dissenters like him were experiencing at the time from the English state.[23] Given what we have just seen with regard to the historical context of 2 Timothy, Paul could have said the same thing to Timothy. Paul and the church in Ephesus were facing enemies from without the church and enemies from within. The situation clearly called for courage, stalwart leadership and a wise head.

A high pneumatology

Unsurprisingly, the apostle emphasized, right at the beginning of 2 Timothy, that the only way Timothy could hope to stand firm was through the power of the Holy Spirit. For Paul, ultimately only the Spirit of God can make a person adequate for all the challenges of the Christian life, especially those of leadership in the church.[24]

The structure of the first eighteen verses of the letter clearly highlights this emphasis regarding the Holy Spirit. Similar to his normal pattern at the outset of a letter, Paul sends a greeting followed by a thanksgiving.[25] In this case, the thanksgiving leads directly into an admonition to Timothy to use his Spirit-endowed gift or gifts and not give way to fear.[26] Closing the passage is a second admonition about the indwelling Spirit: Timothy is to guard the faith "by the Holy Spirit who dwells within us."[27] Also tying together the passage is the word "ashamed" (*epaischynomai*): Timothy is to rely wholly on the Spirit's power so that he will not be ashamed of the gospel. By implication, Paul himself is doing so, and so is not ashamed. Paul's Ephesian friend, Onesiphorus, who repeatedly visited him in Rome, is held up implicitly as an example of one who also relied on the Spirit's power and so was not ashamed.[28]

In 2 Timothy 1:6, Paul begins from the basic fact that Timothy is a genuine believer. As such, Paul can assume he has at least one gift of the Spirit for service in the Body of Christ.[29] Although the

---

23 *The Correspondence of John Owen*, ed. Peter Toon (Cambridge: James Clarke, 1970), 174.

24 For Paul's teaching on the Holy Spirit, see the fabulous and exhaustive study by Gordon D. Fee, *God's Empowering Presence: The Holy Spirit in the Letters of Paul* (Peabody, MA: Hendrickson, 1994).

25 2 Timothy 1:1–5.

26 2 Timothy 1:6–7.

27 2 Timothy 1:14.

28 2 Timothy 1:8, 12, 16.

29 See Paul's argument in 1 Corinthians 12.

apostle does not name Timothy's gift explicitly, it clearly had to do with preaching and leadership in the local church. This is made clear by Paul's later admonitions to Timothy to teach those in error with gentleness and to preach the Word.[30] Paul specifically urges Timothy to "fan into flame" his spiritual gift. The verb "fan into flame" Paul uses here does not imply that Timothy has so neglected his gift that it has to be fanned into flame from dying embers. Rather, Paul is likening Timothy's gift to a fire which needs constant stirring to be kept at full flame. Paul is concerned that given the dangers of persecution and heresy, Timothy may give way to timidity and not be as zealous in the exercise of his spiritual gift as he could be.

Paul can exhort Timothy to employ his gifts because the source of these gifts is not Timothy's own inner resources but the Holy Spirit, whom God has given. Paul states this in verse 7, "a spirit not of fear but of power and love and self-control." The word translated "fear" here, or "timidity" as some translations have it,[31] actually has the connotation of "cowardice" and was often used in battle accounts. In the words of Gordon Fee, it describes "the terror that overtakes the fearful in extreme difficulties."[32] Paul is reminding Timothy that the One who has gifted him for ministry, namely the Spirit, is not One who will lead him to neglect his gift and run away from his responsibilities.

The Holy Spirit whom God has given to his children is characterized by three traits. First, he is a Spirit of power, one who fills believers with power to live for God and his glory, no matter the circumstances. This empowering comes not from the believer's own resources but lies in the inexhaustible strength of the divine Holy Spirit. The Scriptures frequently mention the Spirit as a Spirit of empowerment.[33] In Acts 6, for instance, Stephen is described as a man "full of grace and power," whose words, when he bore witness to Christ, were irresistible because of "the wisdom and the

---

30 See, for example, Paul's words in 2 Timothy 2:24–26; 4:1–2. Towner argues that the "gift of God" in view here is the Spirit himself. See Towner, *Letters to Timothy and Titus*, 457–460.

31 The KJV and ESV have "fear," while the NIV and NASB have "timidity."

32 Fee, *1 and 2 Timothy, Titus*, 177.

33 Consider, in addition to the texts discussed below, Zechariah 4:6–9; Acts 10:38; Philippians 1:19; Ephesians 3:16.

Spirit" with which he spoke.³⁴ Again, in 1 Thessalonians 1:4–5, Paul is confident that the Thessalonian believers are enrolled among God's chosen people, because when he was preaching the gospel to them he was conscious that the Spirit was driving home the truth of his words to them and bringing them under divine conviction. The Spirit's power quickened the apostle's words and applied them to hearts of his audience. Similarly in Romans 15:19, Paul defines his ministry as one which does not deal with mere form and ritual, but results in powerful Spirit-wrought conversions.³⁵ These three texts reveal the biblical emphasis that genuine ministry is accomplished not by human strength, but through the powerful, empowering work of the Spirit. So, it is no surprise that when Paul comes to exhort Timothy to fulfil his ministry, he stresses the urgent need for Timothy to find his source of strength in the Spirit of God.

Second, the Holy Spirit is a Spirit of love. It is the Spirit who promotes "self-sacrificing, affectionate service" to others.³⁶ Again, this connection between the Spirit and love is characteristically Pauline. We have already seen this in Romans 15. We are reminded of Galatians 5:22 where Paul lists the fruit of the Spirit—the solid evidence of the Spirit's indwelling presence. Love heads the list and, from one perspective, defines all the other characteristics. It will take love to truly deal with those who are promoting error. Look at the way Paul spells this out in 2 Timothy 2:24–26. The Christian leader, "the Lord's servant," must be able to engage those in error with firmness, but it must be done with kindness, patience and gentleness. He also needs to pray for opponents of the truth—that God would give them an opportunity to repent and embrace the truth.

Third, Paul states that the Spirit is a Spirit of "self-control." The Greek word here, *sōphronismos*, has taken some commentators by surprise, for it is a term that is regularly used in Hellenistic manuals of moral behaviour. The word itself occurs nowhere else in the New Testament, although various cognate words do appear in the

³⁴ Acts 6:8, 10.
³⁵ Clark Pinnock, "The Concept of Spirit in the Epistles of Paul" (PhD thesis, University of Manchester, 1963), 126. This thesis is an admirable exploration of Pauline pneumatology and is a contrast to some of Pinnock's later work.
³⁶ Kelly, *Pastoral Epistles*, 160.

Pastoral Epistles.[37] However, the surrounding context is extremely Pauline in emphasis: none of the terms listed in verse 7 are regarded as the result of mere human effort, but all are the fruit of the Spirit. Here, in this third trait, Paul is emphasizing that the Spirit is One who enables the believer to make sober judgements and to keep his or her head in fearful situations—both of which were especially appropriate for Timothy given his situation.

What we have here then is a deep appreciation of the believer's and the church's vital need for the Spirit to fulfil the task of mission and ministry. Without the Spirit's power, love and self-control, all is vain. Like Timothy, believers in every age must trust in the Spirit's power as they seek to live lives that glorify God. Paul is arguing in a fashion similar to what was written in Deuteronomy 20. In the context of spiritual warfare, the believer's trust must be in the Lord the Holy Spirit. If this is so, what we have is evidence of a high pneumatology in which the Spirit is implicitly lauded as God, for the believer's hope and confidence is never directed to any but God alone.

The Spirit of the crucified and risen Lord

In view of the spiritual resources the Spirit has given Timothy, Paul now urges his dear friend "not [to] be ashamed of the testimony about our Lord, nor of me his prisoner, but share in suffering for the gospel by the power of God."[38] The key word here is "power." Paul has just told Timothy he can have confidence in using his gift for God. The One indwelling him, who is the source of this gift, is a Spirit of power. Now, Paul calls Timothy to be loyal to both the Lord Jesus and to himself, the Lord's prisoner. It is an appeal, which, if Timothy responds positively, will inevitably involve humiliation and suffering. But this humiliation and suffering can be borne if Timothy relies on "the power of God." This is the power which God gives through his Spirit.

It is absolutely vital to note that this is a paradox, which Paul enunciates in greater detail elsewhere in his letters. The Spirit's power does not eliminate suffering and weakness—rather it manifests itself *in* weakness. Without agreeing with all James D.G. Dunn

---

37 See Kelly, *Pastoral Epistles*, 160.
38 2 Timothy 1:8.

has written, surely Dunn is right when he states that for Paul:

> Weakness does not hinder or prevent the manifestation of power; on the contrary it is the necessary presupposition of power, the place wherein and the means whereby divine power is revealed ... power does not drive out weakness; on the contrary, it only comes to its full strength in and through weakness.[39]

In 2 Timothy 1:9–10 we read a further reflection on the power of God. Timothy can wholly rely on the Spirit's power. It was that power which was at work in the crucified Christ, "rendering death ineffectual,"[40] and revealing life and immortality. Implicit in the statements of these two verses is the paradox just noted: God's most powerful work, the salvific work of the cross, was accomplished through the utter frailty of his Son. Paul puts it this way in 2 Corinthians 13:4, Christ "was crucified in weakness." Yet, in the midst of the Son's weakness, the Holy Spirit was powerfully at work. Therefore Paul can also say in 1 Corinthians 1:23–24 that Christ crucified is for "those who are called, both Jews and Greeks... the power of God." Suffering and weakness by no means imply the absence of God's Spirit. On the contrary, they are *the medium* in which the Spirit delights to work. Since the Spirit indwelling believers is the Spirit of the crucified Christ, the same pattern can be seen to be at work in believers. This is the power of the Spirit displayed in the midst of human weakness.

Onesiphorus, a Spirit-filled man

Paul has urged Timothy not to be ashamed of the gospel. Paul states that, solely because of grace and the Spirit's power, he himself is not ashamed.[41] To further encourage Timothy to trust in the Spirit's power, he gives the example of Onesiphorus. Unlike Phygelus and Hermogenes who were ashamed to be associated

---

39 James D.G. Dunn, *Jesus and the Spirit: A Study of the Religious and Charismatic Experience of Jesus and the First Christians as Reflected in the New Testament* (Grand Rapids, MI: William B. Eerdmans Publ. Co., 1997), 329.

40 Fee, *1 and 2 Timothy, Titus*, 180.

41 2 Timothy 1:9 and 12.

with Paul the "criminal,"[42] Onesiphorus "was not ashamed of [Paul's] chains." Unlike his earlier imprisonment in Rome, when he lived under house arrest in a locale known to many,[43] Paul appears to have been imprisoned in a cell not easily found. Onesiphorus had to expend much energy searching for the apostle.[44] When he found Paul, he was not content with a single visit. Again and again he visited Paul, risking arrest and imprisonment himself. But Onesiphorus was "not ashamed."[45] Why not? From the verses that precede—which we have already looked at—one can only conclude that Onesiphorus' courage was because of the power of the indwelling Spirit. Onesiphorus stands as a model of the Spirit-filled, Spirit-empowered man.

Notice further that Paul is not ashamed to acknowledge that Onesiphorus refreshed him. At a basic level, such refreshment would have involved food and other means of practical help.[46] But on a deeper level, it would have entailed the Spirit-given joys of Christian fellowship. As Dietrich Bonhoeffer (1906–1945) has rightly noted in his spiritual classic *Life Together*: "The physical presence of other Christians is a source of incomparable joy and strength to the believer."[47] In fact, as has been noted above, a key reason for the writing of 2 Timothy was Paul's desire to have Timothy come to Rome to see him before he left this world. Twice near the end of the letter, he reiterates this desire: "Do your best to come to me soon"; "Do your best to come before winter."[48]

Did Timothy go? Did he heed Paul's admonition and overcome, by the Spirit's power, any fears of associating with Paul? We do not know the answer for sure, but there is a tantalizing verse at the close of the Book of Hebrews, where the anonymous author tells his readers that "our brother Timothy has been released."[49] It appears quite likely that Timothy, empowered by the Spirit, did indeed go to Rome, and there he experienced imprisonment for

42 2 Timothy 1:15; 2:9.
43 Acts 28:30.
44 2 Timothy 1:17.
45 2 Timothy 1:16.
46 Towner, *Letters to Timothy and Titus*, 483.
47 Dietrich Bonhoeffer, *Life Together*, trans. John W. Doberstein (1954 ed.; repr. New York: HarperCollins Publishers, n.d.), 19.
48 2 Timothy 4:9, 21.
49 Hebrews 13:23.

the sake of the gospel. Timothy showed himself a true disciple of the Lord Jesus and a true friend to his mentor, Paul, and as such, wholly committed to the Pauline mission.

STUDY GUIDE | *Application & reflection*

1. This chapter speaks of new covenant warfare in 2 Timothy. What is he referring to? What other verses in the Bible speak of this conflict?

2. In 2 Timothy, Paul is instructing Timothy about various issues. Describe some of the issues that were going on in the church in Ephesus. Why was this concerning to Paul?

3. Paul explains in 2 Timothy 1 how important it is for Christian leaders to stand in the strength of the Holy Spirit. In what ways does Paul encourage Timothy to not be timid? How was Timothy to use his gifts?

4. The Holy Spirit is characterized by three traits, according to this chapter. What are these three things and how do you see the Spirit at work with these traits in your own life? Do you ever try to do "the work of the Spirit" with your own efforts? Give a specific example.

5. Suffering and weakness are the experience of believers on this side of heaven. While we see the power of God often at work, we continually experience weakness in sin. Briefly explain this paradox.

6. Paul speaks of not being ashamed of the gospel and then goes on to give the example of Onesiphorus. What are some reasons we might be tempted to be ashamed of the gospel? How does Paul counter those reasons? What gave Onesiphorus courage?

"I believe, to the apostle Paul
the greatest trial was not to be a missionary."
—Kanzo Uchimura

Conclusion

Much of this book has been focused on Paul's letter to the Romans, exploring six essential aspects of the Pauline mission. In the final chapter of this remarkable text, Paul pens greetings to an extensive list of Christians in Rome:

> Greet Priscilla and Aquila my fellow workers in Christ Jesus, who risked their own necks for my life, to whom not only I give thanks, but also all the churches of the Gentiles. Likewise greet the church that is in their house. Greet my beloved Epaenetus, who is the first fruits of Achaia to Christ. Greet Mary, who laboured much for us. Greet Andronicus and Junia, my countrymen and my fellow prisoners, who are of note among the apostles, who also were in Christ before me. Greet Amplias my beloved in the Lord. Greet Urbanus, our fellow worker in Christ and Stachys, my beloved. Greet Apelles, approved in Christ. Greet those who are of the household of Aristobulus. Greet Herodion, my countryman. Greet those who are of the household of Narcissus who are in the Lord. Greet Tryphena and Tryphosa, who have laboured in the Lord. Greet the beloved Persis, who laboured much in the Lord. Greet Rufus, chosen in the Lord, and his mother and mine. Greet Asyncritus, Phlegon, Hermas, Patrobas, Hermes, and the brethren who are with them. Greet Philologus and Julia, Nereus and his sister, and Olympas, and

all the saints who are with them. Greet one another with a holy kiss. The churches of Christ greet you.[1]

This text illustrates the type of multi-ethnic, socially diverse communities that God used the Pauline mission to establish in the Mediterranean. But it also informs us about the heart of the gospel, which is found in the phrases "in Christ Jesus," "in Christ" or "in the Lord." This is one of Paul's favourite descriptions of being a Christian. It is a powerful pointer to the fact that at the heart of Paul's mission was his preaching about Christ, crucified and risen, the revelation of the glory of the Triune God. Only in Christ is there peace with God. Only in Christ can God be served aright.

This Christ-centred gospel is as much needed now as it was when Paul first proclaimed it nearly two millennia ago. Likewise, the six elements of Paul's mission, which have been explored in this book, are equally needed now for the church's mission. Central to the Christian mission must be:

1. Conversion to Christ;
2. Love for his church;
3. Unflagging zeal to win the lost for whom Christ died;
4. Fervent prayer to the God revealed in Christ;
5. A band of brothers and sisters dedicated to one another in Christ;
6. Devoted dependence on the Holy Spirit, the great Agent of all mission.

---

[1] Romans 16:1–16.

STUDY GUIDE | *Application & reflection*

1. Read Romans 16:1–16. What are some things that strike you about this list?

2. Write a list of some believers you are thankful for and why. Are there ways you can encourage any of these people this week and in the coming months?

3. What are the key takeaways you have from going through this study of Paul and his mission?

HERITAGE
SEMINARY
PRESS

Dominus Deus fortitudo mea | The sovereign LORD is my strength